A LEAF IN HIS EAR

ACKNOWLEDGEMENTS

I Want to Be a Poetess of My People was first published as a cyclostyled pamphlet by the National History and Arts Council of Guyana in 1976. A more elegantly printed and designed edition with additional poems was published by the Guyana National Service Publishing Centre in 1977, with illustrations by Harold Bascom.

My Finer Steel Will Grow was vol. 31 no. 2, 122nd release of *Samisdat*, Richford, Vermont, published in 1982. Unfortunately, the pagination of printed copies is faulty, so it is possible that either 'For Walter Rodney' lacks its final page, or 'Love, love' lacks its first page.

Bones was published by Peepal Tree Press in 1988.

The uncollected poems appeared in *Dawn* (1973); *Heritage,* nos 1 & 2 (1973); *Kaie,* nos 12 (1975) and no. 14 (1976); *Independence 10: Guyanese Writing 1966-1976*, Georgetown, National History and Arts Council, 1976; *A Treasury of Guyanese Poetry*, ed. A.J. Seymour, 1980 (GTM Fire Insurance, publication); in *Trinidad and Tobago Review*, vol. 6, nos 1&2, 1982; in *Kyk-over-Al*, no. 40 (1989), no. 42 (1991) and 45 (1994); and in the *Toronto South Asian Review* (vol 5, no. 1, 1986). A good many of the poems have never been published before. Most come from a typescript from which the poems that appear in *Bones* were drawn.

MAHADAI DAS

A LEAF IN HIS EAR

COLLECTED POEMS

PEEPAL TREE

First published in Great Britain in 2010
Peepal Tree Press Ltd
17 King's Avenue
Leeds LS6 1QS
UK

ISBN: 9781900715591

Printed in the United Kingdom
by Severn, Gloucester,
on responsibly sourced paper

MIX
Paper from
responsible sources
FSC® C022174

Supported by
**ARTS COUNCIL
ENGLAND**

CONTENTS

Uncollected Poems (1973-1994)

PUBLISHER'S NOTE

This project of collecting Mahadai Das's poems was agreed with her a few months before her death. Unfortunately, she never had the opportunity to revise any of the poems or to give her considered decision on what ought to be included or excluded. This left a difficult decision to make about editorial principles. Different people urged different approaches. I vacillated between selection and inclusiveness. In the end the collection errs on the side of the latter, though I excluded two weak early poems, 'Haunted' and 'Change' where the printed texts were so defective as to hinder access to meaning. Denise DeCaires Narain Gurnah, who provides a most insightful introduction, went through similar swings of view, but came to a similar conclusion.

There is no way Mahadai Das's work can ever be other than an unfinished project, and I think that readers need to be trusted to see what is absolutely essential and fully accomplished in her work, what is the work of a young writer finding her voice, what was written in politically difficult times and betrayed by history, and what amongst the later poetry might have been revised to good effect if her health had been better. Both Denise and I shared, in the end, the view that the excitement we'd had in seeing the poems become tighter, better crafted and more signal in voice was not one that should be denied the reader. There is scarcely anything within the collection that lacks some sign of Das's fertility of imagination. I also felt it important, with respect to the broad range (and sometimes eccentricity) of her subject matter, to respect her determination not to be pigeon-holed in terms of ethnicity, gender or poetic styles.

There are at least a couple of poems in *I Want to Be a Poetess of My People* that I know Mahadai Das felt embarrassed to have written, but she never asked me to omit them, and it felt like an act of censorship to do so. There was a period (c.1975-76) when she was a young and enthusiastic member of the cultural corps of the Guyana National Service, one of the several conscriptions of the Guyanese people to serve as foot soldiers in Forbes Burnham's tragic and corrupted experiment in decolonisation. There are other poems in that first collection that can only be read with a sense of irony – the poems about the misconceived and disastrous attempt to revive cotton cultivation at Kimbia – but there is always something else in them: startling images and a genuine response to the landscape of the hinterland. By 1978, Mahadai Das was a fierce opponent of the ruling party and supporter of Walter Rodney and the WPA's attempt to forge an ethnically united opposition, as the poems in *My Finer Steel Will Grow* indicate.

The poems in *Bones* were selected from a much larger typescript. In retrospect, I think the original choices were generally sound with respect to giving *Bones* a unity of focus, but there are some fine poems that were omitted at that time and it is a sad pleasure to make them, and the later poems published in *Kyk-over-Al*, available in this collection.

In general, no changes have been made to the texts of previously published poems, except for correcting some very obvious typo-graphical errors, omissions or confusions of punctuation. The sequence of the published collections is preserved; as far as it was possible to determine, the uncollected poems are organised by date of publication.

Jeremy Poynting
January 2010

9

INTRODUCTION

DENISE DE CAIRES NARAIN GURNAH

Mahadai Das is perhaps best known to readers of Caribbean writing by her poem "They Came in Ships". Focused largely on the arrival of Indian indentured labour to Guyana, the poem has been anthologized widely in collections of Caribbean poetry and particularly in anthologies focused on Indo-Caribbean experiences and culture. Indeed, its title was used for one of the first comprehensive collections of Indo-Caribbean prose and poetry, *They Came in Ships: Anthology of Indo-Guyanese Prose and Poetry*, edited by Joel Benjamin et al (Peepal Tree, 1998). *A Leaf in His Ear*, which gathers together Das's published work as well as many unpublished pieces, indicates that her contribution to Caribbean writing is much more substantial than this "representative" poem suggests and her passions more intriguingly diverse. The poems collected here are characterized by a restless determination and energy as well as by unexpected and startling imagery. Amidst the air of sorrow that permeates many of these poems, there is a sharp wit and a keenly reflexive intellect at work sifting through the joys, disappointments, frustrations and pain of a life lived through the fervour of nationalism and the bitter realities of independence in Guyana under Burnham and the mass migrations that followed. The poems in this collection, written between 1976 and 1994, vary significantly in terms of their poetic accomplishment but together they offer unique insights into the construction (and destruction) of an idea of nationhood and into the precariousness of alternative sites of belonging, especially for the woman poet. The trajectory her work charts from nationalism to disillusionment is not uncommon amongst Caribbean poets; what is distinctive about Das's oeuvre is that this shift is so dramatically and decisively mapped. This, along with the spare (I am tempted to say "jangling") dissonance of her poetic voice and the intensity of the work, make hers a powerful and unique contribution to Caribbean poetry.

Mahadai Das's life, perhaps more than most, was shaped by dramatic events. Born in 1954 in Eccles, a village on the east bank of the Demerara river, her mother died while giving birth to her tenth child in 1971, leaving Mahadai, then seventeen, with considerable responsibility for her siblings. The family remained in Eccles where Das's father, Tilokee, was a rice farmer. In 1973 her brother Patrick disappeared while in the Guyanese jungle and was never heard from again. In 1971 Das was crowned "Miss Dewali" and in the early 1970s she also studied at the University of Guyana and was recruited to the Guyana National Service, spending time on the site at Kimbia (in the upper Demerara Berbice area). The mini-biography provided at the end of her first collection of poetry, *I Want to Be a Poetess of My People*, published in 1977, asserts the range of her interests cheerily:

> University student, teacher, beauty queen, Mahadai, up to October 1975, was a member of Guyana's leading para-military force – the Guyana National Service. She served as a pioneer in the Service's hinterland development and is intensely interested in music, drama and dance. (p.28)

By the late 1970s, as Burnham's regime became more tyrannical, Das became involved with the Working People's Alliance (WPA), a party which sought to represent the concerns of farmers and other workers and to avoid the race-based politics which characterized the ruling People's National Congress (PNC), as well as the People's Progressive Party (PPP) and the United Force (UF). By the time her second collection of poems, *My Finer Steel Will Grow*, was published in 1982, Walter Rodney had been assassinated, resistance to the Burnham regime had become a perilous activity and Das was studying in the US. In the preface to this second collection (published by an avowedly dissident press, "Samisdat") Das explains her refusal to use a pseudonym:

> I would prefer my own name ... I will probably be safe for a few years, as the Guyanese government is busy gunning down dissidents at home.

Das returned to Guyana when her studies in philosophy at the University of Chicago were interrupted by illness and she had to have open-heart surgery. In 2003, while in Barbados for medical treatment, she died of a heart attack; she was 48 years old. A life sketched in such stark terms may suggest a body of work marked by the tragic but, while there is a tragic vein in many of Das's poems, there is also intense passion, energy and wit and a patient commitment to her craft.

As the title, *I Want to Be a Poetess of My People*, announces, Das's early poems assume an active, visionary role for the poet as well as a clear sense of the constituency being addressed. The speakers in these poems declaim "newer patterns of meaning" to be found in Guyana's land and people following independence from colonial rule: "This land has bequeathed you new meaning" (p.28). The labour provided by enslaved and indentured people, so violently misused in the past, is recognized as a powerful resource to be redeployed to shape the nation. In "Look in the Vision for Smiles of Harvest" the speaker describes her own labouring body, alongside hundreds of other cotton reapers dressed in the green of the GNS uniform, "Each pair of hands going back and forth, from plant to bag/ in artistic precision, from bag to plant" (p.30). Unlike the exploited labour of the old rice-planters described in "Your Bleeding Hands Grasp at the Roots of Rice", the labour provided on the Kimbia cotton plantations is presented as contributing to the future of *all* Guyanese, rather than the ruling class. In "On Events that Occurred at Kimbia", Das insightfully suggests that patterns of colonial domination were so ingrained in Guyana that they had sedimented into a form of *superstition*, requiring a jolt for a truly national culture to be engendered:

What if people, with their hands stuck from their ears
And tongues laughing outside their mouths,
Would jeer away the threat of superstitious domination? (p.37)

"Militant" makes similar claims for the transformative necessity of change, "I want my blood to churn/ Change! Change! Change!/ March!" (p.39), the drumming beat of the poem underscoring a sense of the people being *drilled* in marching *and* in a politics/poetics of revolutionary change. In the rather spectacularly titled, "Does Anyone Hear the Song of the River Wending its Way Through the Jungle?", the speaker likens the people to "a dark river that flows through the jungle" in a metaphor suggesting the organic wholeness of land and people:

> These same gentle waters have diluted the blood of unnamed
>   heroes,
> Can tell its tales of quiet suffering never quilled on paper
>   memories.
> These same veins of water flow through the land –
> Like blood vessels through the flesh of my mother –
> Can tell of childless logies at the edge of fertility,
> Nigga-yards barren of one single beat of a drum,
> British Guiana evening skies untampered by its silent
>   surveillance
> Of anguish. (p.37)

This conflation of blood with the natural world of land and rivers is a recurring trope in the collection, offering a powerful alternative to the more usual significance of "blood" as indicative of "natural, ancestral" ties. Rather than constituting community via ethnicity, "the people" in these poems are linked by their labour on the land, guided by a Leader who is presented as visionary, determined, and gentle. It is easy now to read these poems as embarrassingly naïve. We know how Burnham's vision for the co-operative republic of Guyana turned out: violently oppressive, racially partisan, economically austere and thoroughly corrupt. But anyone of Das's generation will remember well the initial excitement surrounding the Burnham government's rhetoric of national pride and self-reliance in challenging colonial hierarchies of race and culture (hierarchies perpetuated locally by middle-class Portuguese, Chinese and Indian Guyanese who all established exclusive "cultural associations" which continued to function well into the 1960s). I know I do. Das's willing involvement in and endorsement of the GNS was a bold refusal of prevailing narratives of ethnicity which saw the GNS as a crude method for engineering racial integration. Popular stereotypes prevailed of an Indian community overly concerned to protect the virtue of "their" women from supposedly sexually predatory African Guyanese men. As is now widely documented, GNS *did* function as an institution in which the abuse of women (Indian women, but others too) was not uncommon and it is evident that vindictive racial politics often dictated how conscripts were treated and who was conscripted in the first place. But these historical facts shouldn't eclipse Das's impulse to be part of a project with the *potential* to transform the atavistic status quo of racial politics in Guyana. This impulse is there in the first poem in her first collection, "They Came in Ships", which offers an account of the arrival of Indian indentured labourers to Guyana but while the speaker proudly links herself to this history , she is also careful to acknowledge other figures from that historical moment (Cuffy, Akkarra, Crosby and others) and to remember "logies" *and* "nigga-yards". Das also alludes to class and caste hierarchies at the start of the poem, suggesting that, dislocated from India, the Atlantic crossing unsettles these hierarchies. The speaker does look backwards but the emphasis is on "Seeing beyond, looking ahead" (p.26).

In *My Finer Steel Will Grow*, there is a marked shift away from the bold visionary stance and muscular physical presence that character-izes the speakers in her first collection. Instead of a powerful Soviet-style peasant-poet with blood churning as she strides through her country, these poems are whispered, not declaimed, and images of fragile, embattled bodies abound. Exuberant "vision" is replaced by a guarded watchfulness and the poems become knotty, secretive and introspective with no clear sense of who is being addressed. Instead of the ornately descriptive titles of the first collection, many of these poems are untitled or, where titles are used, they are cryptic and withhold "clues" to the poem's meanings. Psychic rather than geographic landscapes are invoked and the poems are allusive and densely metaphorical; "Untitled II", for example, begins, "There are eyes that watch behind/ the shroud of darkness. The cancerous/ prey is frantic" (p.48). The speaker of the title poem presents a body under siege from within (by parasitic fleas) and without (by an unidentified aggressor, "hammering/ rains the bullets"):

> I will drown my fleas or the river
> choke me to death. They pound
> like a carpenter gone beserk (p.49)

The verb "hammering" suggests both attack and a forging into shape (the "finer steel" of the title), conveying the sense characteristic of this collection, that poems are forged out of painful struggle. In another poem ("Untitled IV") the speaker shivers in her "inadequate skin" and is "unarmed against the sky", her heart "a handful of tissue" to be protected from "the guerilla air" (p.51). In four untitled poems (V-VIII) a disappointed speaker addresses a "love" that might easily be aligned with a beloved person or a beloved ideal.

Das's choice of images are powerful and unexpected: "the limbs of my whispers climb wearily/ the steep sides of your sternness"; "your back/ a keel of stone bruising the red lake/ of my womb" (p.56); "Come into company./ Upon each jammed window, ease your love" (p. 47). A haunting sense of unfulfillment echoes through these poems, most memorably in an image of the barren woman:

> Place your torch upon this cave
> that cries
> bringing down the roof of my emptiness
> to a flat, silent shore where waves
> visit (p.59)

Interpretive possibilities flicker and fade and flare up again in these poems and resonate powerfully, eluding attempts to anchor the poem's meaning in the "facts" of Das's life (unrequited love? her bitter disappointment with the failed "revolution" in Guyana? her painful illness? transplantation abroad?). By contrast to the uncertain voice and vulnerable body of the female poet-speaker, Das describes the bloated corpulence of political tyrants, "those with paunches and their contented belches" (p.52) who bear responsibility for murdering their opponents (Walter Rodney and the Jesuit priest Father Darke are specifically referred to). Interestingly, when Das wants a strong image of resistance for a government "grown corrupt", she invokes an Edenic image of Guyana's hinterland:

> In this forest of green and great dreams,
> in the unvanquished footsteps
> of our first pride, we tread;
> with our string of beads and our naked
> spears we come with our shield of courage
> to repossess
> our native waterfall. (38)

Amerindians, routinely excluded from political processes in Guyana, are presented here as the rightful claimants to the land and are associated with an ethical, small-scale way of life in direct contrast to the manipulative over-consumption of the Burnham regime. The degree of naturalism (and optimism) in this image is unusual in this collection, but it establishes the spear as metonymic of resistance, a trope that in other poems Das can deploy with economy (see p.52 and p.53, for example).

The introspective impulse of *My Finer Steel* is intensified in Das's third collection, *Bones*, as is the focus on the female body. In some poems the body is pared down to its skeletal frame while in others it *exceeds* its human frame and becomes monstrous. Many of the poems reflect on the vicissitudes of being a woman poet and express deep-seated anxieties about being heard/read. In "Unborn Children", the speaker mourns her barrenness in terms that align "unborn children" with "unflowered words". "Sonnet to a Broom" with which the collection opens celebrates the humble broom but

17

also invites parallels between the invisibility of domestic work and that of the poet whose work "retire[s] unpublished to the dark/ spaces which my closet keeps, secretly" (p.65). The broom was the election symbol for the PNC in the 1961 elections along with the slogan against those with colonial sympathies, "sweep them out and keep them out", but the poem does not appear to directly refer to this. In the title poem, Das with characteristically sharp wit uses the popular phrase "skeleton in the closet" as a pretext for reflecting on the conventional paraphernalia of femininity (prom dresses, red pumps, veils and petticoats). The gaunt, jangling bones are presented as flute instruments desperate to tell their tale: "They have no wish to stay in the attic./ They want to be part of the world" (p.66). The poem concludes with an image of the notes produced by these "bone flutes" "rising/ helium balloon forever" (p.67), an image of transcendental "other worldliness" which recurs in the collection and surfaces in the many poems which anticipate escape from the limitations and pain of embodiment by embracing death. In "Resurrection", the speaker comments wryly on the ultimate futility of obsessively maintaining sexual modesty:

> Maggots crawled through my hair,
> between my teeth and eyes,
> ate at places, which, in life's profane vanity,
> I guarded with passion and suffering. (p.72)

Again and again, Das presents the female body as disjointed and fragmented, a direct consequence of its over-idealized status. In the long poem, "For Maria de Borges", Das offers a sustained narrative of the ways that the body of the woman migrant in the metropolis is exploited relentlessly for labour (of all kinds) so that she is reduced to her working parts, "I am a pair of hands/ A pair of feet" (p.82), and her selfhood violently truncated:

> into the real world I come
> with my muscles pumped
> so you may drain me

with my feet polished, shining,
my feet ready. (p.88)

In her passionate indictment of the commodification of the migrant woman, Das draws on and extends Sylvia Plath's exposure of the impact of an exploitative patriarchal system on women; Plath's "The Applicant" for example, concludes, "A living doll, everywhere you look./ It can sew, it can cook,/ It can talk, talk, talk" (Plath, *Collected Poems*, pp. 221-2). Given a prevailing culture of prescriptive, restrictive femininity, Das and Plath, in their distinct ways, seem to suggest that the woman who wants to *write*, rather than *inspire* poetry must necessarily invest in a robustly challenging poetic identity. The speaker in "The Growing Tip" makes precisely this argument, boldly delighting in the monstrous images and gritty realities of the manuscript she sends to the publishers:

What she sent reminded no one of a garden:
Pieces of skin, a handful of hair, broken
Teeth, bits of glass – an iron chest, rusty, grim … (p.109)

Delight in confounding the decorum expected of the woman poet – indeed, of "the poetess" of Das's first collection – is tempered in *Bones* by poems that are more elegiac and tentative in spirit. In "Flute", which recalls the bone-flute of Amerindian mythology, the speaker presents the body as a frail instrument which "can scarcely hold/ this rhapsody" (p.104), while "Oars" describes the poet paddling the river's depths with the "slender oars" of her words (p.112). Interestingly, too, "Oars" opens with the line, "I am an Indian woman" before going on to suggest not the "East-Indian" woman the reader may have anticipated but an *Amerindian* woman "with long hair,/ a band of beads across my forehead" (p.112). There is a sense here of Das deliberately side-stepping her "received" ethnicity as the basis for poetic identity. This is further consolidated by the fact that there are so few specific references to Indian-Guyanese culture in her work (apart from "They Came in Ships"). The poem "If I Came to India", in *Bones*, may tantalize with the

19

promise of a return to "roots" but it is constructed as a series of possibilities posed as questions to which answers are not provided.

Das might easily have offset her disappointment with Burnham's independence programme by investing her creative energies and consolidating her poetic identity in Indian cultural forms. But she chose not to. The previously uncollected poems now available in *A Leaf in His Ear* confirms this. The conspicuously small representation by and of Indians in Caribbean Literature (particularly shocking given the fact that Indians in Guyana are a *majority* of the population) may well make it tempting to claim Das as a representative Indian poet. But this would be to ignore her persistent avoidance of the lure of ethnicity and her embrace of creativity and poetic craft as avenues to wider horizons. An uneven and rather sentimental poem included in the Uncollected Poems, "Sea Waif", might endorse this point for, while there are recognizable elements of Das's own biography in the poem, these are carefully mythologized using ballad and fairy-tale forms suggesting a deliberate avoidance of "the facts" (of ethnicity, location and so on). The addition of the Uncollected Poems (written between 1973 and 1994) also allows the reader some reprieve from the terse compactness of *My Finer Steel* and *Bones*, softening the edges of Das's poetic oeuvre in places and filling in the gaps in others. There are delicate poems here of love lost and found and experiments (not all successful) with poetic registers and forms, notably ballads and sustained narratives. Two early poems written in Creole, "Me and Melda" and "Chile is Who Yuh Fooling" suggest directions not pursued elsewhere in her work, though both poems offer representations of a distinctly Indian-Guyanese Creole. In the opening lines of the latter, a father warns his child of the risks of upward social mobility:

> Chile,
> Is wha yuh trying fo reach?
> If Gad did want we touch de sky
> Every day
> Yuh na tink he would a mek am low? (p.117)

A Leaf in His Ear allows the reader to see the full range and breadth of Das's poetic interests and abilities and her intense engagement with the craft of poetry. The poems vary in style and achievement and there is a strong sense of a poet arrested in mid-flow. But there is excitement and energy too in this collection in witnessing the drama of a poet coming to voice, veering from the expansive declamations of her first collection to the secretive and terse introspections of her second and third collections. Two quotations will serve as conclusion here to convey a sense of the poetic range and power of Mahadai Das's oeuvre. The first is a contemplative reflection on the poet at work at home, in "Blackout":

> The city hulks in blackness,
> its forms arresting my blind stare
> as I sit in its judgement
> from my table of illuminations,
> with my scribner's ink, my cheap
> paper; recalling early country darknesses,
> the sooty juglamps of childhood. (p.97)

The second, an untitled poem quoted in its entirety, from the Uncollected Poems, conveys Das's ability to startle with the precision and resonance of her images:

> Look at me:
> when you speak,
> mountain ranges
> rise inside me. (p.166)

I WANT TO BE A POETESS OF MY PEOPLE

(1976, 1977)

THEY CAME IN SHIPS

They came in ships
From far across the seas
Britain, colonising the East in India
Transporting her chains from Chota Nagpur and the Ganges plain.
Westwards came the *Whitby*
Like the *Hesperus*
Alike the island-bound *Fatel Rozack*.

Wooden missions of young imperialist design.
Human victims of Her Majesty's victory.

They came in fleets of ships.
They came in droves
Like cattle.
Brown like cattle.
Eyes limpid, like cattle.

Some came with dreams of milk and honey riches.
Others came, fleeing famine
And death,
All alike, they came –
The dancing girls,
Rajput soldiers – tall and proud
Escaping the penalty of their pride.
The stolen wives – afraid and despondent.
All alike,
Crossing dark waters.
Brahmin and Chamar alike.
They came
At least with hope in their heart.
On the platter of the plantocracy
They were offered disease and death.

I saw them dying at the street-corners
Alone and hungry, they died
Starving for the want of a crumb of British bread
And the touch of a healing hand.

Today, I remember my forefather's gaunt gaze.
My mind's eye sweeps over my children of yesterday
My children of tomorrow.
The piracy of innocence.
The loss of light in their eyes.

I stand between posterity's horizon
And her history.
I, alone today, am alive,
Seeing beyond, looking ahead.

I do not forget the past that has moulded the present.
The present is a caterer for the future.
I remember logies
Barrack-room ranges
Nigga-yards.
My grandmother worked in the field.
Honourable mention.

Creole gang, child-labour —
Second prize.
I remember Lallabhagie.
Can I forget how Enmore rose in arms
For the children of Leonora?

Remember one-third quota
Coolie woman.
Was your blood spilled so that I might reject my history?
Forget tears in shadow — paddy leaves.

Here, at the edge of the horizon
I hear voices crying in the wind.
Cuffy shouting – Remember 1763.
John Smith – At least, if I am a man of God,
Let me join forces with black suffering.
Akkarra – I too had a vision
Before I lost it.
Atta – in the beginning, I was with the struggle.
And Des Voeux cried
I wrote the Queen a letter
For the whimpering of the coolies
In their logies would not let me rest.

Beaumont – Had the law been in my hands.
And the cry of the coolies
Echoed around the land.
They came in droves
At the door of his office
Beseeching him to ease the yoke off their burden.
And Crosby struck in rage
Against the planters
In vain
He was stripped naked of his rights
And the cry of the coolies continued.

The Commissioners came
Capital spectacles with British frames
Consulting managers
About the cost of immigration.
They forgot the purpose of their coming.
The Commissioners left,
Fifty-dollar bounty remained.
Dreams of a cow and endless calves
And endless reality, in chains.

CAST ASIDE REMINISCENT
FOREHEADS OF DESOLATION

I want you to know…

That you have helped build this land,
That your curved back in the fields revitalised sugar.
Brought forth, out of your womb a new industry
Of waving paddy leaves.

Cast aside your apologetic philosophy of uprooted destiny!
No bride regrets her entry
Into the arms of her husband.
Yet, she never ceases to love her father.

Of this new union
She creates the offspring of a new vision,
Recreating old meanings
in age-old patterns
Woven by all ancient civilisations,
Never stolen, never broken,
But forever weaving newer patterns of meaning.

Cast aside reminiscent foreheads of desolation!
Did you not come across the seas
With a dream in your heart
Of love and contentment unshackled by grief?
Today your loaded arms of silver,
Tomorrow, your multicoloured raiments,
Yesterday your tears of motherhood.

This land has bequeathed you new meaning.
She is your husband.
No wife regrets her married state!
How else could she savour

the fruits of motherhood
And rest benignly in love's glade?

Today your Khukru-Beras tingle
And glitter in the midday sun
And your mali lies contentedly
Until the dusk, when love's fingers
Will unravel the dawn.
Your breasts, like jars of blue-jamoon wine
Will yield their succinct flavours.

Tomorrow you will rise
And robe yourself in pleated glory to welcome the dawn.
Evening shadows of logies will soon pass away –
No hybrid-headed whips will taint your husband's dreams.
No more will blind magistrates look at you
And see white smiles beyond you.
Crosby has not died;
His spirit will live on to protect you
From a prostitution of womanhood.
Sing your lullabies!
Cradle the gifts of your womanhood serenely!
Tomorrow,
No more ships will come across the seas!

LOOK IN THE VISION FOR SMILES OF THE HARVEST

In the cottonfields
Five thousand acres of cottonfields
I stood
Two woman's hands, an empty rice-bag around my waist
Two eyes surveying the forest-fringed horizon
Around me. Hundreds of reapers
Green backs bent
Green backs bent
Each pair of hands going back and forth, from plant to bag
    in artistic precision, from bag to plant,
Routing the boll of whitened silver, fruit of a dream
Born two hundred years ago
When Magdalenenburg bled with aborted fertility.
Here I stand
The palm of my brown hand shading two gleaming eyes
    from the richness
Of sunlight overhead.
Here I stand and survey all around fruit born of frustration and pain
And hope.
Here I stand on my own soil.
Five months ago
I watched us trample yesterday's cruel baboons with the
tractor and the plough.
The baboons – they have retreated into the forest.
Listen...
At the end of the day of sun in my hair
Cotton in my hand
Sun on my back
Cotton around my waist in a fifty-pound bag.
Listen...
When the darkness falls around this Kimbian jungle
...like a cascade of tenderness
...like a mantle of love...
Hear the eerie cries of baboons of desolation driven into the forest.

Listen to their whimpers of subjugation, of lost dominance.
Look around you,
See the tired bodies resting on layers of beds.
Awaken at dawn
And, like a silent shadow, move towards the darkness;
Watch the mist clear your lungs;
Run towards the sun, awakening to the beauty of life and,
    rising over the jungle,
Stop and watch the mist retreat before the sunlight.
Once again, at eight, move into the fields of dreams.
Plough and sow your songs – the thought you thought yesterday
About my grandfather and yours
That you wish to give your children, and mine in its maturity.
Think of your child of tomorrow passing through this now jungle
Reaping the fruits of your hands, and sowing for tomorrow's children,
Today, your hands rough and scarred, your forehead lined –
Look in the vision for the smiles of the harvest.

YOUR BLEEDING HANDS GRASP THE ROOTS OF RICE

Silently I move in a vision of lost happiness
   in a world forgotten.
Old woman,
Where you sit, feet planted, day by backbreaking day,
Your bulging waist weighed down by the coppers in your apron-pocket,
Do you know that I have changed?
Old man,
With your dry coconuts, that look each like every one,
   each day of each year,
Like any other year —
Don't you sense evolvement, misty-slow, painful, like new death?

A fruitless climb to a barren star,
You sell your picky-picky, scrawny chickens each day.
You weigh them in those old, broken-down scales.
Don't you know as you touch the scales —
One buys, one dies?
Do you know your backyard is fertile, brown earth?
When your fingers knead the soil for my flat belly
And brown wrinkles multiply — one by one — they add the age
To your sunken
Sockets
For my stomach.
Do you know my shoes stand on a wasteland
While your twisted toes squeeze, in a frenzy, the squelching mud
That will bear you your life?
Your bleeding hands grasp the roots of the rice
In my fields,
And the seed of life you delved into the earth
Has sprung up to mock me.

LOOKING OVER THE BROAD BREAST OF THE LAND
I SAW A DREAM

I saw a dream in the distance,
A rooted dream. A green dream.
There were beautiful branches
Vibrantly green, verdantly green.

I rose to meet that dream
And I looked over the broad breast of the land.

I saw fields of fertility
Fields fed by the rain
Fields fed by the sun
Chimneys rising to worship the sun
Acres of listening corn
Acres of answering pine.
And I saw the harvest beckoning the reapers,
Children laughing in the sun,
Girls strewing their dreams with flowers;

The evening wind like a messenger of love
Lingering a kiss on each white boll
In the blue light
Of the falling
Night.

And there were ships that came from other lands;
We filled their arms full of our fruits.
As laden holds turn to greet motherlands like lovers,
The acquiesced teardrops
Fell no more into the ocean,
While tall on the sunlit horizon, stood glimmering
Promises of return.

I saw my children dancing in the beams of moonlight,
Weaving patterns they spun with the threads of their yesterdays
Of black shadows hanging over the river,
Coppers winging the air from cane-sugar's palaces,
And, on the loom of tomorrow,
I saw them weave benab cities in the forest,
Molten factories drinking deep from waterfalls feeding
    visions sailing downriver,
My children, in universities, born and grown in the jungle
Like a symbolic womb, cradling and nurturing the generations
    of yesterday's visions.

DOES ANYONE HEAR THE SONG OF THE RIVER
WENDING ITS WAY THROUGH THE JUNGLE?

Make me a poetess of my people.
Let me, too, drink the sun that shines in early morning
Knee-deep paddy-fields
Drinking droplets dewing on endless acres of cane.

Their life is like a dark river that flows through the jungle.
No one hears
Or no one listens when a gurgled protest of beauty escapes its
    brown throat;
Civilization motors her way into the quiet songs of billowing
    cane-leaves.

These same gentle waters have diluted the blood of unnamed heroes,
Can tell its tales of quiet suffering never quilled on paper memories.
These same quiet veins of water that flow through the land –
Like blood vessels through the flesh of my mother –
Can tell of childless logies at the edge of fertility,
Nigga-yards barren of one single beat of a drum,
British Guiana evening skies untampered by its silent surveillance
        of anguish.

In the full breast of the forest, there lives a hunter, his
    wife, his sons... his daughters.
By the fall of night, he and the jungle are one.

The logger has camped three nights among his trees.
But it rained.

Four years now, the porkknocker –
Seeker of unfulfilled dreams –
Seeks that golden materialism.

His dreams, borne on the back of the evening wind, are lost through
    the forest.
At harvest-time, the reaper in the field celebrates the harvest alone.
The sweat of the cane-cutter fertilizes next year's groceries.

Their life is like a dark river that flows through the jungle.
No one hears the song of its wending.

So no one listens.

ON EVENTS THAT OCCURRED AT KIMBIA

Blood spouted from the dark brown rivers.
The earth opened in a crack of fear
To hold unwillingly their treasures of gold and silver
Near the huge kumaka tree.

Where are the ladies — lily-white —
Crouching in black fertility?
Where are their men waking in a sun-child's slumbering womb?

Their spirits, it is said, jealously guard their centurian treasures.
Till now — though long powerless with the crash of crowns —
They hold sway o'er men's rural minds.

But what if folk would set superstition aside?
Cast it away, like a deadly snake, from them.
Where would then be their masters' power of invocation?
What if a revolution thundered along this path
And trampled their disintegrating psychic forms of domination?

What if people, with their hands stuck from their ears
And tongues laughing outside their mouths,
Would jeer away the threat of superstitious domination?

The babes would walk the night armed with courage,
Fearing no unseen force.
The girls would sleep at night,
Untortured by dreams of fatigued imaginations.
The men would rise up, rediscovering themselves
To construct new visions for tomorrow.

THIS IS KIMBIA

This is Kimbia
Where the raging march of the soldiers
Rides the waves in the beat of a drum.
Hear the drum – is the sound of the jungle echoing the
Cry of baboons at night –
The pre-dawn symphony's sound.
Hear the fingers of a strumming player
As night
Courts the moon with her starry eyes.
Here
The Dutch man with his sunken treasures
Was buried with a white dog by his side.
Here
The haunts of the Christian friends
Were torn by the bulldozer's teeth.
Here
The ancient forested lineage
Gave their sinews for the heart of a town.
Centuries resurrected cotton.
Cotton, in glee, brought the mills.
Mills, surprised, fetched the ships.
Ships came, revising history's watery course, wending its way
Through the palatial green.
This is Kimbia
Where the raging march of the soldier sounds the trumpet-call
For the thousands,
Young hearts – riding the waves in the beat of a drum.

MILITANT

Militant I am
Militantly I strive.
I want to march in my revolution,
I want to march with my brothers and sisters
Revolution firing my song of freedom.
I want my blood to churn
Change! Change! Change!
March!
We are the army.
We are the people.
We are Guyana marching for change.
This revolution's banner is clasped by our hands.
This revolution's banner will march through our feet.
This revolution's banner will march through our feet.

Singer I am
Singing I strive.
I want to sing my country's revolution
I want the notes to climb Pakaraima's peaks,
Spread like her stars o'er Kimbia's peaks,
Grow, like seeds, in our people's hearts.
I want to sing
I want to sing
I want to sing my country's revolution.

Writer I am
Writing I strive.
I want my words scorching pages
Burning tongues
Paging my people's servility.

Dancer I am
Dancing I strive.
I want to dance through patterns of pain
Beaded to rooted, furrowed brows
Of our sons of the land.
I want to be a son of my land.

You and I are posterity,
In our veins run atoms of gall,
Atoms of gall,
Cane-sugar's ever-running historic stream.
In history's sad march
Was I ever a son of my land?
Now
I want to clench the stain of my earth in my palms.
Seeds that I planted
For my child to nurture
Will shoot forth through my soil,
My earth,
My land,
My country.

I want to feel my country's agony.
Throes of a bloody birth!
A scream of life!
A fertilized dream!
Child of the revolution!
I want to grow... grow... grow!
I want to grow for my revolution.
I want to march for my country!

AKARA, DID YOU HEAR US MARCHING?

O Akara
O Akara,
Did you feel the drum of our hooves climbing over the sun
Over the trail
Over the sand
Over the storm?

O Akara,
Did you hear our wail in the night
For the blisters
For the sores
For the red bruis'd soles – the dying edge of the song,
And the search – Oh the search for the blazing light of the moon?

Over the miles
Over the miles,
Oh the march was long but the song was not wrong
As each day it saw with its hundreds of eyes
The light at the edge of the dawn.

O Akara
O Akara,
Did you hold my hand through the black night
The blind night
The endless dark night
The lonely hours of the dawn?
When at length we marched in the joy of night
Did I hear you sing your song in the brilliance of light?

HE LEADS THE PEOPLE

In the era of the people
I stand astride the excitement of reconstruction.
Eagerness is a sparkling ray in my eye
The blood races through my veins.
Thoughts of tomorrow dart around my head
Reconstructing structures so newly mounted
They gleam in the sunlight.

In the era of the people
The horizon beckons the vision to rise, like the morning sun
In the sky.
And in the forefront of battle
He leads the people
Tall, his vision communing with the light on the horizon.
Beautiful hands, that caress so gently
So firmly, those hands reconstruct.
Clothed in jungle-green, like the forest
And as silent,
He leads the people.

These years are for the people
These songs they sing are mine.
And in the years ahead
He stands
A guiding light
Brighter than any other
But nevertheless, a guiding light.

Holding the clues, he forges ahead, beckoning the followers,
Knowing over the horizon stands the vision – bold and bright.
And the people, wearying
And maybe footsore in the future,
Chant the songs of hope.
In his jungle-green attire as green as the forest

And as silent
He forges ahead
And as silent
He leads the people.

MY FINER STEEL WILL GROW
(1982)

UNTITLED I

There was always the urgent essentiality
and the meeting of hearts.
There was, too, time wickedly playing
games; the scent
of a certain flower. Consequently,
I write: in retrospect, I speak
to you.

UNTITLED II

There are eyes that watch behind
the shroud of darkness. The cancerous
prey is frantic
as he seeks to desist the springing.
But crouched in bitter wait
for all the blood that spills – like stars
that fall to death –
there will be a resurrection of stars.
A coup will take place and stars,
armed to their shining eyes, will guard
our right to walk unfettered
through the streets of heaven.
There are eyes that crouch behind
the shroud of darkness.

MY FINER STEEL WILL GROW

My heavens are hailing upward tonight.
The felled star is like a dagger
stuck deep in my heart. Anon. I am gone.
There is no place to rest
my accidental head.
It is a dog's life. Today there are no bones.
Yesterday there were too many.
The common fleas irritate my hairy nape.
My legs are poles the world
cannot keep upright – they
dare not fall though
my paws trace out this path
of death too often that I smell.
My snaky hunger obsesses,
my red-eye rage,
apoplectic, twists my growling gut.
Yet
the day will come when the sun
will shine its brazen face
upon my heart, gone dark
like night and rotted blood.
I will drown my fleas or the river
choke me to death. They pound
like a carpenter gone
berserk; hammering
rains the bullets
on my back.
Whilst the hammering arm
in rhythmic falter flags,
my finer steel will grow.
My heaven.

UNTITLED III

Birds break through the wall of heaven
and everywhere angels
are chained to darkness.

Now that the prince's sceptre has rusted
and the legs of his gilded chair totter –
even now the heavy clank of chains
is heard in his cellars.

Ah yes! the government of heaven
has grown corrupt:
my passage to earth's eden
is laid with fire.

Spider! who has wickedly woven
your thistled network of shadows,
hung your knotty schemes upon
our guileless and warm branches,
beware!
In this forest of green and great dreams,
in the unvanquished footsteps
of our first pride, we tread;
with our string of beads and our naked
spears we come with our shield of courage
to repossess
our native waterfall.

UNTITLED IV

How soon the cold rain, pellets
shattering the thin grass.
Shivering
in my inadequate skin, I inside
huddle pondering a sudden treason,
a ransom that unprepares: a watch
unconsidered.

Unarmed against the sky, the earth
bears barren limbs; inarticulate arms
that hide origins. This heart
is a handful of tissue I must coat
in warmth before the guerilla air.

WHILE THE SUN IS TRAPPED

While the sun is trapped
in clouds of heaven, tiny guerilla lights
border the moon.
Hardship bends the back of the wind.
Loneliness carves a philosophical man
celebrating his despair. The air
is cruelly shot with the tyrant's glee.
But the day to come crouches, holding
his long spear in the night.
Ah, they hold to prey the man
and his starving child.
Like the bullfrog who croaks, they
bare their teeth and prepare for the slaughter.
While their fangs drip
with the blood of priests and the aborted
day, while yet the lords
of the fallen leaves lie yellow
in their coming and moist rot, while
those with paunches and contented belches polish
their cars,
the vengeance of heaven waits armed
in the shadows.
The sun comes up in a coup
for the golden day.

MY FINAL GIFT TO LIFE

Death would be my final gift to life.
Then: if I must die, I must.
Let the progeny of stars light my path to heaven.
'Me' will be one more star to fiercely light
the darkness of this land.
This body will bear the final calamity.
I will not be the fish caught
in his wily net.
I will not touch his rotting sceptre beaded
with murder,
nor eat my bread in a crumbling house overrun
with rats.
All over the land is heard the sound of women
weeping; the muffled voice
of children starving in the drought.
Who can inhale the stench of wickedness
or dwell whole in this leprous air?
In their sad coat of mange, dogs
hang their hungry heads.
The night is pierced by strange cries of woe,
but he who stirs their tears
in the cauldron on his vanity,
preparing for a feast and a night of loud song,
little knows he of we who
sharpen our spears in night's
naked hours.
Death be my final gift to life.

FOR WALTER RODNEY & OTHER VICTIMS

Weep not for your child.
Others are dying yet.
Saints are struck down.
Murderers are raised to ugly statues
whose wicked square
razes the grass to stony ground,
vilifying the air,
and birds escape to greener spaces.

O Mother, mother,
as you spend the pennies of death
upon those hollow eyes,
remember a man gunned down,
his guts that spilled their clandestine sin.
As you place this coffin into ground
and tears give way to final rites,
there is another
beside you. She
is weeping yet.
Of her children there are three
open faces who do not understand
a father split, like a butcher's corpse.
Framed by their metal-heavy ring of guns,
silently she sits
upon the stone
of her grief; she holds
a pair of bombed-out limbs
hacked by the sudden blow, the treachery.

Tears fall
where I sit.
All the leaves of the trees are falling away:

naked stems stand alone; charred,
strung-out limbs
seeking to span the bitter wind that comes.

Mother,
he who plays chess with our lives,
growing fat on good wine and Cuban cigars,
he who rides to bed by limousine
chartering quick rides to his city seat, he
is living yet.
While our purses of freedom grow spare,
their daily lives spent hour by dimmer hour;
the wind of death but shakes the flame.

UNTITLED V

O love
you silence my words leaping
to their long tongues of flame, spent
like arrows of intent upon the wall
of silence in your eyes.
Subdued
as a roar to the glowing embers of uneasy breathing,
the limbs of my whispers climb warily
the steep sides of your sternness.

Spreading in all directions they come,
my love's tendrils growing across
your great shoulder.
My words are new leaves that constantly
bear fruit, little red flowers facing
the open high sun of love.
But your wall is a bitter garden
where my roots are not fed; your back
a keel of stone bruising the red lake
of my womb. All my years
are spread upon you, yet
you harshly slam the shutters of my eyes
against love's lighted window.
My roots, feet of fear, plant them-
selves warily in other ground.

You watch me wither, your cold
indifferent eye like a moral:
my fallen flowers are blind
testaments that enter the great womb
of rest, in a silence.

UNTITLED VI

Love, love, I have survived so long
upon the naked bed of your unconcern.
But I am learning your roster:
the bugle call at dawn,
your gate-shutting rites,
the changing of the guard.
Circumspect inside, you inspect
your pleated ranks, the chessmen
from your peopled platoon stuck
upon the iron squares of your strategy.
You sit, your chin
upon your hand, like history,
contemplating boundaries.
But only new time
can be your adequate mistress.
The days are miserly, the hours
thin and vapourless, the new season a dream.

I am the insurrection
your strong hand put down; the cry
and the blade in the sunlight,
the nascent moon-threads
of the garment of dreams,
the unpaged history of you and I,
the beautiful moon-child
whose cry I always hear.
They have not dealt with me yet: your squad.
Their bullets get wet, they
change their guards. Had I stood
against the wall of my courage,
or had they fired at the dutiful
hour, it would have been
final.

I would have won
the case of my belief.
Instead, this
wretched sentence exiling me
to memory.

UNTITLED VII

Place your hand upon my womb,
upon that which covers itself
so well, that shelters love's
hurt tunnels in its bone-strong
care.
Place your touch upon this cave
that cries
bringing down the roof of my emptiness
to a flat, silent shore where waves
visit: but I have always beckoned
the great sea
to come and reclaim me. Caress
the walls of my longing
for each wet swell soothes me.
Feed me with your fertile streams
so my banks may swell to greater sphere
until, until
new cries celebrate new comings, love's
bright bulb-hanging pendants
testifying light.
Rest your ear upon this secret room
that waits, that calls
like distant music for closer ears.
Come into company.
Upon each jammed window, ease your love.
Lay a ring of flowers round my door;
leave them to grow.
I shall water them.

UNTITLED VIII

Awaken my love.
In the distance, conches
cry.
Let us rise, gathering our skirts
about our knees.
With a song we will plait our hair.
The sun's rays shall be our morning bangles.
These delicate wrists of morning light shall sustain us.
Let us sling our pails
upon our arms' strong rods
and dance to the well.
Our men will still be sleeping
while we stoke the fire. The coals
will leap like joy in our hearts,
to flame. Our lords will wake
to hot curries and fresh-baked
wheat.
And while it is yet dark, they
will make their way to the fields.

THE DAY OF REVOLUTION

I dreamt that the day of revolution would come;
that thousands would storm the city streets
screaming for justice.
Who can hold back the climbing sun in the sky?
Children hate the trapped darkness of the night.
I heard a cry echo the wind...
Soon the crowd advanced and raised
a further cry.
Like full-blown trees
at their maturing, the schools
surrendered their eager fruits. Then
the Bastille storm advanced upon
the scampering rats
like an irrevocable flood,
like an irrevocable coming of dawn.
Ordered to march, the soldiers, my brothers, came
bearing in the stems of their guns, flowers
for the children of freedom's
new regiment.
The counterfeit general, left wingless
in the hostile air, clothed in the tarnished
brooches of his vanity, unprepared
for the sudden speech of freedom,
continued to spin his illusions
with the rotten yarn of his life.
Last night
I dreamed that the day of revolution would come.

BONES
(1988)

SONNET TO A BROOM

Your frayed teeth must take away the grey dust
fallen from daily reams of urban dreams.
Edges unsullied by your tasks, you sweep
where musty remains of heaven seeped, till
you gain only a clean floor of truth
which leaps before Ruth's lace, untainted by
the polluted dust and dirt of weeks.

You retire unpublished to the dark
spaces which my closet keeps, secretly,
uncalled, until once more, in despair, I
must dare you now to clear away the grime
accumulated through your absent mime.

Yet unreproachful, you return to use,
efficient though abused, but willing.

BONES

Grotesque jewels, they hang
in my closet beside prom dresses
and red pumps.

When petticoats are sleeping,
they continue to jangle.
They make a strange noise.
Moonlight shadows their gauntness.
Pumps and brogues are blind to their squeals.

Veils thin to a fringe on their bony blades.
They could tell a tale.
They want a say, without doubt.

Long ago, they were supply fleshed.
But then, all meat fell away
from the bone. Some teeth
and hair remained.
Someone should examine their story.
After all, it's not that they dwindled
into dust altogether. Besides,
these bones could make more than music.
They're a fire-tried instrument.

They have no wish to stay in the attic.
They want to be part of the world.

Oh they are hungry for wind to sing
through their tissue, so hungry.
They wait for the earth at the plough.
After winter's fallowness
and all its severity,
when earth is torn up
by the diligent farmers,

when golden seedlings
offer
love to their heavens,
they wait without praise or reprimand.

So when these white flutes
send a note out – a golden apple
from the Mexican border – it takes to air,

full shape climbing,
          rising

helium balloon   forever.

CHICAGO SPRING

Chicago winters are grim.
Like apostolic messengers,
Spring and Summer revelations
slight love's hard absence
upon the wintry ground.

Hooded shadows
wrap themselves into night.
Rainsticks, slender-snaked,
hang from resolute limbs
of staid office-racks.

The air's complexion
is as grey as a corpse.

Reluctant as sunlight,
Spring peeps upon low turrets
of the neighbourhood, and March
air chills stay on like unwanted
guests after supper.

Old ladies march through late
April promises, secure in winter's
garb. Old men tote umbrellas.
                    Careful girls
tuck sweaters into shoulder-bags,
and guys wear jackets anyways.

There is a lack of faith.
April comes: shy sunshine, limping
showers. Chicago trees, naked atheists,
unfrozen still-life from a recent past,

will not usher the season's green poetry,
its baptismal blossomings.

Love comes tripping into tulips...
a springflower dancing
in rain?

Scarfed against sun's slanting light,
a wintered unbeliever won't
pluck it, for his unthawed eyes.

UNBORN CHILDREN

I mourn unflowered words,
unborn children, inside me.
Who attends the funeral of the desert rose,
wears dark rags and solemn faces
for the doing-away of the unborn?

O widows of old Greece with your black shawls!
Raise your voices with their seasoned sorrows
to my invisible funerals.

RESURRECTION

Triumphant, from dark days of starvation,
I rise from the grave,
blood thin, body weak, will too exhausted
to claim glory for my victories.

Instead, in the subdued twilight of this summer-eve
of my resurrection, I ponder my history.
I see it in sullenness of roofs,
the droop of the willowtree.

I raise my eyes to the sky, flesh of the universe,
wan in bloodless whiteness.

The moon's fullness, its perfection, the deep
significances of its circles, elude me.
It is too round. My beliefs stick faster
with professors of worlds, penny-like and flat.

It is more than faith or fear
which makes me say on a day like this,
that I may easily fall off
the edge of the world. Unlike Columbus,
I am neither helmsman nor sailor
but I pass from adventure
into some profound reflection of a past
which may gain me entry into future's night.

I dwell upon my entombment,
clear, unmarbled walls,
coffin-like spaces with no room for my limbs.
Its futility is darkness's prism.

I dwell upon my undertakers' faces,
their elevated hopes that I may rest in peace.

I recall their incantations
for the redemption of my soul,
the sprinkling of holy water upon my dead face,
the sign of the cross nailing me under.
How mercilessly they pinioned my dreams
on earth's calvary!

They dressed me in white linen
to moulder into dust and worms.
Impurities festered in my tomb.
Their rejoicing
was unaccommodated by death's dark world.

In my burial-robes, they adorned me
with jewels from junkshop disposals
and backyard sales.

These survived putridity
of worms in their jubilee days.

In earth's opaque jar, hair,
bones and my teeth remained.

Maggots crawled through my hair,
between my teeth and eyes,
ate at places, which, in life's profane vanity,
I guarded with passion and suffering.

They behaved as children,
sucking at my unmothered breasts.
They dared to kiss lips which, at heights
of enmity with death, were only his.

They dared these impunities.

When I rise from this tomb
as if I were Jesus come again to proclaim
to the world that death has been conquered,
I come with joy in my breast,
but without exultation.

Though my visage be sombre as a judge's,
my eyes, those of one going steadfastly
to the gallows, I have no fear of death in me –
I have returned from the abyss.

I understand the libations
at the feet of gods.

Though I have reason
to blow trumpets, I play
an elegiac flute in silver hours
of a misty morning, calling birds with songs,
early grasshoppers, awakening the population
at your farm.

I draw the sun out of his milky horizon
with invisible strings, as if I were a puppeteer,
and with my skill, I engineer the morning.

SONNET TO NEW FLOWERS

In the rectangular and tall absence
Of the builder's art, wrecked tenements stand,
Bricknude, aggressively banded against
lewd lack of tree, flower or friendly hand.
Windows with broken glass stare, token
gazes sent from iron-fisted buildings.
In desolate air, indifferent haze,
Hate stares in gunshot-interrupted
Silence. Black flowers materialise late
from the dark, wounds in their sides.
Here, in this arena of smoking eyes,
dope, and hounds among poor-inhabited
tenements, hope, absent watercan, has
never lent itself to flowers.

HORSES

All the pink-coloured horses are coming in.
They gallop in from the sunset, hearts
beating like a drum.

Unbridled, they canter,
Flushed. Approaching twilight.
Behind, Sun is a blaze of metal
Sinking into the sea.

Where are the golden horsemen?
They too are drowning.
They will rise from the sea tomorrow.
Their dust will rise up from the east.

Meanwhile, the horses come in,
last troops in the twilight,
with their hoofs of steel, their wild manes.
The drums from the Amazon are thundering and
breasty women are blowing into the fire.

The children are petulant, sucking their thumbs
with outcast expressions.
It is suppertime and their stomachs are groaning.

But outside the hut, the men
are hammering the goatskin drums with their fingers.
They wait for the horses to come in.

FOR ANNA KARENINA

Crushed in the snow, she lay,
her blood splayed on the iron tracks.
Steeped in falling winter's whiteness,
in death, without a tear.

Gone that softness that curved
in his hand so recently. Gone
without a murmur from lips
which kissed so passionately.
Gone that heart that beat
insistent, fierce.

Where is that fine passion now,
that pinnacle in one life,
that intricate clockwork in the breast?

A woman's broken body remains
robbed of its sweet, wild breath.
In being robbed, passion could
but flee, for its badge must
be worn but well.

DECEIVED OR DECEIVING

I want this day to finish quickly.
Tomorrow must seize me by the throat.
If it doesn't today will hang me
from a tree by sunset behind that hill.

With this bitter root I chew,
sunset sinks into morning.
Sun rises only when I sleep.
Winter seizes me
while summer trees are abundantly green.

My eyes are autumnal. Yellow
leaves drop to the ground
as blazing Greek chariots bear the sun
with his golden horsemen
across the world's roof.

I knock on your door at midnight.
When you come, it is but air
which greets you.
I constantly sing my songs for you,
but you cannot hear them.

I write on this page
but the ink is invisible.

I take my confessions to every shrine
I know. Gods do not listen.
They watch my anxious face
with stony eyes.
Not a gesture will they make.
I walk up aisles to high altars,
kneel at each god's feet carved in stone,
wood or marble, hang rosaries in adoration

as requested, pour libations upon royal feet
of clay, swirl incense round fixed heads,
touch holy fires to my forehead as instructed.

Yet they are dumb.
Their lips may be broken with a hammer.

Were I to hang from my world upside down
like a spider, so that my eyes
stood at my feet, and my toes twiggled
in moist clouds; then, were I to imagine
that in this universal disorder of things
only I was in position,
I would still change,
or be changed, involuntarily.

When you come to me from the roof,
climbing through my multiple windows,
parachuting into my bed at midnight
like a trained soldier or adventurer;
when you leave before you have come,
and arrive after you have left,
I am unperturbed.

Instead, I marvel at your consistency.
I wonder that the world's remainder
is deceived, or undeceiving.

FOR MARIA DE BORGES

I

Death, black moon, high mark
on night's blue canvas.

Stumped shadow beneath the lynching-tree.

A star hangs over me.
Dark sore.
Is it death?

Like a phantom
honed into walls,
I inhabit a city of steel.

Between its iron teeth, mechanical, regular;
in escalators, prisonlike elevators,
I am lifted indifferently, dropped

like a stone,

borne, like a jumbie
beneath stony earth.
Shadowless, I descend, deeply
into nightmares of childhood;
down to steel-lined metros,
to summerheat that beats, insistent,
at my temples. Down, down to carriages,
grimy steel-boxes caging men like packhorses
being driven to a mill.

Down to obsessions caged underground –
down, down, down.

Phantomlike,
I move in long narrow streets.

Down Broadway.
A single head of cattle exiled
from gentle grazings of our pasture.

From whence has this traveller come
with his long hair, his lost eyes?
I am a pair of hands.
A pair of feet.

Eyes without candle.

Bird stricken.

Shrunken globe, my joys,
small circumference.

My token is the same.
Little copper sliver moving me around.
Little city token. Little metal ring.

Expensive little sliver.
Dear metal moon. Small perimeter of dreams.
Small perimeter of dreams.

II

A death-broker awaits me.
He counts his cash.

Slight and weary,
I stand. Tears
trail in the dust.

He takes all my jewels.
He takes all my rings.
He steals my rubies,
my rope of pearls.
He grabs my tiara, my bangles
of silver. He gives me tokens
to send me to his factory,
send me to his store,
cage me in his offices,
keep me in his kitchens.

At gunpoint, he steals rubies in my cheeks,
my full curve of hip.
He bestows me coppers –

so I may buy
a jacket for my shoulders
from his huge garment-store,
hose from his hosiery, wine from his cellars;

so I may purchase a space for my bed,
a closet for my clothing, a space
for my child
and a space for my spouse.

He takes moons from my eyes,
my fingers' nimble gifts –

he hands me rose-coloured glasses,
hard-rimmed, rectangular.

I look through his spectacles.
I see him better.

. . .

Moons in my eyes are lost but to me.
They have moved to another orbit
larger than me. In private
constellations, I only could see them.

Wheeling in wide orbit now,
all may espy them.

They are wheeling round and round
in a luminous light.

Dreamlight ignites them.
An inner light.
Music, cosmos, world:

we are in harmony.

I surrender my tiara of stars.

He greedily grabs them.
He returns
cheap sparkle from his factories,
cheap glitter from his streets.

I go there to buy
things that appear like the real,
spending my life in imitation,
never knowing what's real.

What is real is what I've given.

What's real is a city token.

What's real is the theft.

I am a pair of hands.

A pair of feet.

III

Death rides, high black moon over all my dreams.
Secret rider across sky's low fields.

Sacred shadow beneath the lynching-tree.

Like blue aether, I move
through streets of dreams.

I go to the river's edge
where the moon is real.

To the sea's edge where the moon's
dressed in silver.

I stare at the stony stars.

Waves of eternity wash over me.

I have come to the river.
I have come to the forest.
Forest of jade.
Forest of emerald.
Forest of clear streams in my head.

I am flesh and blood.
I breathe.
I eat like a lion when hungry.
I touch. I caress. I sigh upon another's neck.

I am man, love.
I am woman, love.

IV

Tomorrow, I rise
between dead thighs of another day.
To be bridled like a horse between the hours,
a bit between my teeth, a bruising saddle
on my back.

Like a packcamel in desert terrain,
I will ride, the load of existence
upon my camel's hump, the print
of my hoof in the sand.
... but a wind
can erase my mark, a gale blowing
inland, or a storm.

No hoof's ink may be written
on the sandy dust of this world, no hoof,
cloven or human,

to declare I was here:

that I walked
with another's pack upon my back,
without water for days,
my face bridled with leather.
My shadow is here in the midday sun,
my bridled shadow in the desert sand.

V

The black sun of death
sinks into sky's atavistic dome, where
I stand, invisible to all
but that black judge, mocked
by my nothingness.

This phantom and I,
ignorant, shadowless,
packcamel by day, creature
of moon by night.

                        Locked,
between these hours' iron bars,
sunlight is divested from me –

I, who dream
of being a riderless unicorn,
at sea's edge where the moon is high;

I, who should wear
stars on my wrist, flowers
on my forehead; I,
who should sing like birds,
and like them, fly;

I, who believe in emerald forests,
sapphire skies, ruby rocks, silver seas,
in opal skies, jade stems, coral sea-roses,
rockplants of ivory

curled

within her seabreasts, her hairy forests,
jadegreen seaweeds making mermaids hair
by moonlight;

I who believe in the magical moonrock;

in faeries in dresses of aether;

in the noble prince on a fine horse;

in flowers which converse;

In plants that whisper;

I who believe in the jewelled existence:

sunlight's gold upon each finger,
diamond-spray waterfalls on rock;
the mink coat upon the mink;
the jewelled emeralds of the tiger's eyes;
rainbows after rain.

VI

I sailed upon a Persian rug of dreams,

now sold

in the marketplace,
without my song
or name.

Ah poems of invisible authors!

How many years in the weaving,
this pattern of dreams?

Where, the tightwoven self
buried beneath the counter?

You spend ten thousand on my design.
You spend five.

You admire my motifs.

Can you explain their weft, their warps?

VII

Death is a lonely shadow flickering
through the night. A lonely passage
between birth and beyond.
Secret nightmare.

O song of my voicelessness.

Song in the sand.

VIII

Landscape of nightmares,
city of skyscrapers,
treeless and flowerless city –
city without children.

What has become of Persian dreams,
their neat emblematic borders,
their central motifs?

Bloody splatters stare at me,
the steely knife twisted in the stomach,
the bloodied machete wielded in hate.

Guns smoke.

Muggers
and their hates
await knife or bullet, or both.

Victim reproduces victim by default.

IX

into the real world I come
with my muscles pumped
so you may drain me

with my hands polished, shining,
my feet ready.

into the real world I come
with the hurt in the bone
the agony in the flesh
the vacuous eyes of hours
the feral teeth of the air.

with my coffee and my coffeebreaks.

with my madness at nine, my dash at five.

into the heat of subways, that fester
in my brain.

into mugging at gunpoint
on a night I am most high.

into the rape of the defenceless.

into the lies and into the theft.

LIGHTNING

No desert orchid blooms
in the arid heat of his longing.
No storm thrusts death's door
gaping before his surprise.

Contented as cows
chewing the grassy days of their lives,
they moor always on the same pasture,
sheep with a bell around the neck
to toll comings and goings.

The family choice grows fat
after the birth of her children.

After a flash of lightning,
after a storm, he gave her up:
the woman with hips of flame,
tongue of ivory, breast of red wine.
Lips of ruby.

He no longer dreams of a fierce duel,
a wrestling to exhaustion.

COME BREAKFAST WITH ME

Come breakfast with me, love
as I dress in white skirts of pure morning;
as I step lightly upon the grassy hem of the world;
as summer flowers lend the air their perfume
and garlands of sunlight adorn me.

Put your glass in my tray; fresh orange fruits
of the day, the early croissant, black coffee
with cream.

Let us sit around white tables of conversation,
offering Hegel a roll, inviting Kant to counter.
Let us, wrist upon wrist, finger upon finger,
lips upon chaste lips, sing to each other
with our silent, deep songs,
and our gazes full of birds.

Let us recount our dreams;
jewelled swords and innocent lovers,
unintended wounds and democratic energies...

Let us breakfast together, together, love

in wide white skirts of pure morning.

DIAMOND

Long lost
in their laughing tale
of blue Caribbean waters
or Arizona nightskies; entranced,
a sleepwalker in a privileged vision,
I am dazzled by your blue-diamond eyes.

A mysterious woman
flew from a European winter
with you strapped to her arm
like a late Christmas parcel.
A diamond shone on her finger
like light.

Held securely,
You were marked out by her mark,
She by yours.

Everywhere, in whatever manner
you go, you must wear her sign
like a banner.
                    Alright, medieval
knight. Exhibit your trophy
from your Holy Crusades.

Bear your cross,
a hand against the breast.
Pledge devotion to your Christian sect!

Your cross drives a wedge
between you and my heart
but I wear a blue diamond
spawned from your eyes.

I turn my hand,
examining its ghostly gleam
in the moonlight.

DEPARTING

Departing is simple;
crammed suitcases, a ticket,
a change-of-address...

The future doesn't need a destination.
I have that in your eyes.
In your heart, I have not found a port
but wide-open seas where I may dream.

In your arms, I find not a denial
but wonderful affirmations. Your smile
possesses power to ignite candles
in my heart, and, in your hands you hold
my candelabra of dreams.

Arriving will never be –
unless God has set a date to judge me by.
I am sure he is too busy for that.

So between never arriving and always leaving,
my spirit swings like a pendulum in the clock
of the universe, and were it to unhinge
I would be a bird flying backwards forever.

PAIN

Pain, bunch of black berries
sprouts in a desert of absences.
Love spurned is neither hate,
nor acid grapes.

It is not tears, rain
upon a willow-tree; Ophelias
hanging desolate upon backyard boughs
but ugly dark clouds rumbling without
consideration. It marks a sorrow.

It is not sleepless nights.
It is sleeping upon the skulls of the dead,
each note of music skeletal in the dawn,
mending skullplates for a funeral.
It marks a parting.

It is not remorse –
a single phrase undoing eternity
with its elect poison; swift arsenic
reaching the heart, then lungs.

It is eternity going by without you

a giant parade less one pair of eyes
peeping from a window above...

It is not friendship
transforming flight faster than sound
into a boat with elegant sails on the duckpond –

it is a heart, a blue lake with flamingos'
wings flaming among the weedy banks;
gracious swans on a glassy surface gliding,
reflections considered by the sky.

It is love which refuses to answer
speaking with eloquent eyes.

FOR BRUCE

You are seeking.
I am hiding.
Constant, a flower, a cactus,
I am in the monumental chain of existence,
a link valid as you.

You drive into your past
for seven days, at St. Paul's:
I do not interfere —
after all — who am I to intercept a gaze
draw a kite to the ground
out of curiosity.

You go west —
less a frontier-man advancing
than the approach, with trepidation, of an uncertain bird.
One more of Columbus' crew,
you dream up phantasmagoric savages ambushing
the beach, their teeth of welcome open as day,
a spear in the heart, an armoured hut in the firelight.

BLACKOUT

City lights are out
and robbers are about.
I dare not venture
outside my door.

Inside, sleep is my guest
too late for my early bed.

In darkness
I give you flame,
meditating by your side,
watching you weep, waxen remnant
of a romance turned to dust in a month.

The city hulks in blackness,
its forms arresting my blind stare
as I sit in its judgement
from my table of illuminations,
with my scribner's ink, my cheap
paper; recalling early country darknesses,
the sooty juglamps of childhood.

WATCHING

every approaching footstep betrays
my intentions. It is past three.
In the stacks somewhere, you must
be seated. I could find you easily.

You wish to be alone.
Your absent shape is imperious in the air;
and my frequent glances, squirrels chasing each other.

I have hidden the nuts of other meetings somewhere,
but in the needy time, I have forgotten.

ON DREAMS AND CONSEQUENCES

When, as a child, I fell
from my hammock of dreams,
a brown-feathered bird,
heavensent, flew to my hand.

Calm in my palm,
a ray of sunlight, reflective
without a murmur, it sat
till my tears dried.

I have fallen from many
sun-tasselled dream-canoes since;
and if tears were pearly ropes,
they could measure a
Niagara.

This span of glitter flutters
through blue aether on a winged
mission, chirping into my breast.

As I walked past the wide and concrete
stairs of your city, that black swallow
fell from my eyes, singed by metal suns
of your century, still as a stone.

BIRD

Out flew this bird

on a telepathic
winging to your
shores, from my head.

By homestretch,

it had grown
into a swan

white-fleeced
long-necked,
too heavy now
to fly.

You clipped
its wing, kept
it a pigeon anklestrung,
homefed,
homespun.

SECRETS

One by one, dark chocolate
or infected kidney, I give you
my secrets. Some, I wrap with a red
bow. Some do well in plain paper.
Others are posted. A few lie stealthily
inside that wooden box nailed against your wall.

That public address holds my purposes sealed.
Quiet, small bombs ticking without a clock,
they never explode in the Academy,
only in my mind.

OARS

I am an Indian woman
with long hair,
a band of beads
across my forehead.

I paddle against desire's deep
slow-dark river,
sliding softly along
in love's canoe.

My words, slender oars,
bear my boat forward —
a keel of silk
upon the water.

My fists clenched
round these wooden
spears — I row
consistently.

Ahead —
the river grows
churlish. Rapids
threaten.

My bark of reeds
is frail, light stems —
insufficient.

The current is fierce.
A weariness seeps
into my marrow.

When that time
comes, love,
will you rescue me?

FLUTE

My body's a hallowed
stick of bone, a flute
through which you pipe
your melody.

I am those parallel
eyes of air
along my spine,
which measure
your heavy rhythms
vibrating in my marrow

Play gentle, love,
my frail reed's
single stem
can scarcely hold
this rhapsody.

IF I CAME TO INDIA

If I came to India
shall I be on a broken pilgrimage
to Mahatma?

Resigned or rebellious
at street-corner hunger,
shall I wear penitence, a saffron
robe, the wooden beads of my days
cast about my breast?

Shall I be Methuselah
in my tradition, a foreign vine
grafted to the Deccan Peninsula?

Shall I find
the poet naked on the mountain?
Shall I discover philosophy
in mountain-caves where
Everest reigns?

Near the Tibetan border
where monks levitate, is
the secret of Being written
on a parched leaf?

If I come.
will I find my Self?

BEAST

In Gibraltar Straits,
pirates in search of El Dorado
masked and machete-bearing
kidnapped me.
Holding me to ransom,
they took my jewels and my secrets
and dismembered me.

The reckoning lasted for years.
Limbs and parts eventually grew:
a new nose, arms skilful and stronger,
sight after the gutted pits could bear a leaf.
It took centuries.

In the cave where they kept me,
a strange beast grew.
With his skin of glistening jewels
and his deadly tongue,
even I was afraid of him.

In the dark Ajanta caves of my breast
ever since he has stayed,
with his measure of venom,
his exact poison and scintillating glitter.
At a certain hour, I almost love him.

ENTRY

You did not break down the door.
You did not loudly knock.
I scarce heard your breath.

Like light, you came through my window,
sunny-bright.

Night has fallen, a devil's mantle.
All her candles are out.

The raven croaks in the dark.
The owl, in knowledge waits on a limb
of God's bark.

O Salamander!
Sightless, how can I see you?

SACRIFICE

Trombones of death
Are calling, calling.
Black flag.
Fullmast in the wind.

Breathing a ghastly air,
my beloved, saddled to midnight,
dark stallion, rides.

His eyes burning night's cloth,
he gallops to her altar
cantering to the tantric traces of her breath,
cape streaming in the black wind.

Kathakali, blue queen,
black-nosed Mother of the Cosmos,
Jewess of Death, do not call us.
We are the sons of morning.

She beckons and beckons
offering a necklace of skulls,
a bloodied pair of lips, a sword on hip.
O insatiable Goddess,
mother of the damned,
death will claim us all if we listen.

Entranced,
he gallops to her breast,
eyes fixed to her face.
Behind her back, she hides
her quick sword.

THE GROWING TIP

They sought the 'growing tip of poetry',
its first frail-green shoots
on which to 'ooh' and 'aah'.

They assumed a garden: English roses,
palms of victory high-raised
on a history of thorns, thick
hedges, neatly trimmed.

They assumed a gardener:
a 'Being There' type seeding
and nurturing and coaxing gardening's
lengthy process from seed to flower;
finally, beaming with his gloating,
false pride of parenthood.

They assumed a house
to which the garden attached,
a black leech of thirst upon
an oasis of blood; a benevolent master,
gentle mistress, mischievous, annoying,
harmless children.

Perhaps they assumed a car or two,
a dog, a cat, a singing canary
hanging by its wiry prison on the porch;
a jolly postman, a friendly milkman,
an every-so-often handyman.

What she sent reminded no one of a garden:
pieces of skin, a handful of hair, broken
teeth, bits of glass – an iron chest, rusty, grim…

She told of jungles, of suppers of snakes
and monkeys; of bills evaded by a change-of-address;
of late payments as a matter of principle;
of forgetting genres of old people, babies
and children; of a living-for-oneself philosophy
which led one, like a modern-day Christ
to bear his cross to the Lonely Hill of the Gallows.

Oh she had things that grew –
horns and tails, arms of different lengths,
automatic fangs near bureaucrats, a tail,
(a bit of bother when she wore a dress);
aunts whose heads she preserved in bottles
of pickles on a shelf, a father stoned
by a proliferation of Oedipal daughters –

'Aiee!' they cried, 'What a monster!'
'This is not a plant!' said the editor-chief.
'It's not a tree!' cried another.

'It's not a rosebush!' (they) cried in unison.
'Not a weed!' a shy one piped at last.

A plant from another planet?

Not a plant?

Even as they peeled off postage-stamps,
horns grew right out of each ear!

When they picked SASE out
from its envelope, a tail uncoiled,
(it caused quite a shriek!)

'My God! It grows, it grows,   it grows!'

As they watched,

       in high shock,

from every tip,

       it continued to grow.

UNCOLLECTED POEMS
(1973-1994)

ME AND MELDA

When a throw de remarks at she,
   she duckin',
she playing like she shut she aiz
   dat she ain hear,
but as Gad deh above
   if I lie, slap me down dis minute,
yuh can bet de frack yuh gat on
   de portals a she aiz wide open
an de blood runnin red-mad thru she brains
   an she grindin she teet
bitin' back she tung
   stranglin me in she min'
cause she can' win now
   she gat fuh tek she time an wait
fuh de moment when she gat me,
   dat blasted whore,
      BAP!
in de palm a she han'.
Den… Aye gal
she gan tear out me hair
an' dig out me eye
an' hope
when she done
I ain good fuh no man.

[c. 1973]

CHILE IS WHO YUH FOOLING

Chile,
Is wha yuh trying fo reach?
If Gad did want we touch de sky
Every day
Yuh na tink he would a mek am low?
How lang yuh able sap yuh mout wid napkin?
Every three secan yuh dip yuh mout
In de cup –
De fire-hat cawfee bun yuh tung.
Yuh haul back,
Yuh hand shake, mek de cawfee
Fall in de sausa,
An yuh – sap, sap, sap
Yuh mout wid de fancy papa.

Chile,
Is wha yuh trying fo fine
When yuh force da bitta cocktail down
Yuh throat
An yuh stomach belch am up
And yuh swalla am back
An yuh smile and seh –
'I'd like another, thank you.'?

Chile,
Is who yo trying to fool
When yuh pushing baby pram down de Wata street pave
An lef am stan up outside supamarket,
Tek yuh las five dalla
Fuh buy shoulda bacon an Chedda cheese,
An a touch, touch shampoo
An blue toilet papa,
An wax wrap foil,
When yo baby

Leff outside alone
A halla?

CHILE!
Yuh tink is me yuh foolin?
When yuh family come wid dem Desoto
Yuh killing two, three chicken
An yuh slavin whole day
Fuh mek dem feel nice.
An every half hour yuh sendin a de shap
Fuh Russian Bear, Pepsi and ice,
An yo smile in yuh kitchen
Cause yuh family laughin and gaffin,
An yuh neiba Claris peepin
Thru she dutty winda blind.

But, chile, if yuh see yuh family next Christmas
Yuh lucky, yuh know.
Nex year yuh go start mine chicken yuhself
Dem dam chicken getting too dear
An none a yuh pickney na eat yet.
Wah yuh go do if yuh husban na get wuk nex week
An de fowl-lady come fuh she money?

MYSTERY OF THE NIGHT

Falling shadows of the night descend so softly,
so silently... where I stand
alone beneath these stars.
I stare above, I study the moon
the stars, the trees, the night.

O night, who are you?
A great black veil that hides the day?
A symbol of rest, of peace?
Of calm and placid thoughts?
A friend of natural, unspoiled things?
Preserver of this life?

Night, are you a cruel force,
a softer, darker mask
covering so much turbulence,
so many hidden emotions... so much
that seethes beneath veneers of sophistication
and self-possession?

What are you, night?
A black curtain of mystery
enshrouding the foliage of the trees,
embracing the wild birds and beasts asleep in your hair,
hugging to your breasts the stalking midnight spirits
and moon-drenched lovers,
hiding nature's evils, and yours, so cautiously?

I look at you, night,
that lies below these studs of light
— the silver moon, the jewelled stars
enraptured in the canopy
— the ceiling of these lights
lending more magnificence to the jewelled bulbs of night.

Wherein lies taunting shadows
oversized reflections, frightening thoughts
that haunt the child – the terror
– the night, which stealthy creeps upon the day
into darker hues and blacker shades... of night.

What are you, night,
who leads men on to find your mysteries, your secrets,
causing the young to be enraptured
to envisage your nostalgic romance
or to shudder at your deep, sinister meanings?

And though we cannot penetrate you,
yet you cause us to marvel, to exult
at the beauty you bestow to your helpmate,
the moon and the myriad stars
symbolizing a timeless union
an eternal beauty and tranquillity.

[1973]

THERE YOU LIE

There you lie,
shattered scraps of glass fantasy,
broken fragments of a rainbow heaven.
Where your shadow falls ,
desolation creeps round your forsaken pieces.
You lie alone
friendless in the cold night air
under a cold foreboding sky
where darkness brings shuttered panes and doors
against you.
You have ceased bemoaning your fate,
but why lie you in such isolated aloofness?

Somewhere
Somewhere

there lies another place for you
Truer, more inviting
to warm the coldness in your heart.

[1973]

A LONG WAIT

Every footfall sound is yours
And when it passes my door
I hope and wait for another
Knowing it will be you
And when it's not you
I wait for the morning
And try to hurry away with sleepless sleep.
Such refreshing hope blows through my heart
And the early morning air caresses my body
And the beauty of dew-drenched trees rises above
The quiet house tops.
Now I look out for you.
Each passing object
Each moving man
Become distractions
To keep me from looking too much for you.
Each passing minute
Brings its own excuses fluttering from my mind.
The bells ring.
And that is the crowning explanation.
Until lunchtime
When new ones more impossible
Manufacture themselves
And afternoon
When horrible thoughts
Begin to frighten my senses
And suspicions stifled re-emerge
With the ring of another bell.
And settling into a restless bed
I hop quickly out at a voice like yours
And run, full of hope, to catch a late visitor
But it's not you.
So I must drink my tasteless soup
And my cold tea

And wait a hundred hours until morning
When you come,
If you come.

[c. 1975]

THE FIRST FOOTSTEPS

These are the first footsteps in the dark,
A broken sapling for the land-hungry sailor,
The first footsteps my eyes are treading down
the corridors of my soul.
My hands reach out to touch the tired, mad
old man. Now must my knowing fingers strain
his shattered dreams through tortured halls of time.
But these lines will reach him in the cold,
future night — whilst he is yet asleep on his bed
of sorrow, and while his wife yet prepares for
the lonely funeral. These will smooth away
his troubled brow.
Hard will be the lines.
Bitter the spit of blood in their faces cushioned
still in its own fat.
How can the weary sleep in this storm of cruelty?
Or dance to the white strains of music while
their brothers' blood drains on the innocent grass.
Worded, my cry will echo in their ears — till
they wrestle in their beds of angry sleep — till
they run shrieking in their carpets — dried up
in their martinis — the table for the feast
covered with the gaping blood of my wound.
Bulge will their eyes, red prominent eyes,
pulping in fear of confrontation.
Scattered that cold night will be the dream of the maiden.

[Jan 1978 / July 1979]

CALL ME THE NEED FOR RAIN

Call me the need for rain.
For I am in want of a shower of truth.
I am starved for bread and the milk is too dear.
Call me the need for rain.

Call me the want of sunlight.
For I am hungry for a star but the swine eat husks.
This leprous air.
I am starved for flowers and stars.

Call me the need for rivers in my eyes.
For the pain is so deep tears will not come.
And the want of love is upon me.
Call me the need for eyes.

Call me the need for hills in my heart.
For the land is so flat it is flooding.
And the pestilence is sharpening its teeth.
Call me the need for hills.

Call me the need for storm!
A slant force of angry waters.
Baring my breasts, laying naked my soul.
Call me the need for storm!

Dec 1978 / July 1979

MY BREAD OF STONE

Cold is my bread of stone.
My bitter tea fouls
Its inner course in the duodenum
Of my tears.
Ah! The night rains hard
And there is no shelter.
The cracked back of the sky tells
My upward seeking eyes there will be
A storm soon to prove the weather
Foolers more fools.
Yet, does it matter that
This once green grass is growing
Brown and parched with thirst? That
Fruits, once heaped in their
Abundance, used to beckon, like
The vendor's smile, my coppers,
Shrivelled, now demand my dollars, spare
Like the bones beneath my covering flesh?
Oh! The tender roses in my garden
Are starved of water.
With sad eyes I watch them wilt.
Or the tears dried in the indifferent sun.
Or the blood upon the Dutch-thick wall.
Soon come the day
When flowers will rain from heaven
And the stars will take to wing, and spread
Throughout the night, like light.
And the birds will come out of hiding
And sing upon the growing green.
Soon come the scatter of laughter echoing
All around.
And starlight dwells entrenched in women's
Eyes.
Soon come
Soon come.

[c. 1979]

FOR PATRICK

Great Jehovah,
you let my brother
be lost like a common snail
without mourning.

You let him grow mad,
pacing the iron space
two straight lines confined,
measuring his steps keenly
between impossible parallels
in his life, grieved and bewildered.

Into that primeval and city-forgotten
jungle which dragged him into its own
remembrance, the twin geography of this
world and the next, unwittingly he went,
without even maps of child-young crayon
lines, without the golden compass of
your sure guidance, without your
multifarious light.

Was it his appointed time to fill
that high office I mentioned previously?

Is that why you called him
from all my carefully-constructed
dreams, my sandpapered corridors,
my high-glaze windows?

Or did my desperate brother play,
like Bergman's mediaeval antihero,
a grim game of chess with inflexible
death, and lose?

[c1983/4]

THERE'S A FINISHED PLAY

There's a finished play
typescripted
in my head.

In a large, empty
auditorium, behind
drawn, heavy curtains,
the whole act's
been rehearsed.

'At the climax
the heroine fell,
with all her skirts,
deep into his eyes.

He, a chivalric lover,
eyes masked from the world –

his ready feet in love's stirrups –
galloped in upon the moment,
snatched her up with
a passionate kiss,
to his breast.

Together
they rode
to the land of love...'

But you, sweetheart,
watching me intently,
are you sitting in the wings?

[c. 1983/84]

YOU HAVE RETURNED

You have returned.

Some fount in my heart
is unscrewed; the poetry
flows and flows tonight,
a fall or a fountain,
a forest stream quietly
overcoming stones in
its course.

Love, what were you doing
there, that place so far
away from my heart that
in your absence, my very
blood seemed to run more
slowly, all my tangible
tempos seemed to sigh
and turn away from
implementing their previous
mad, wild dance in my temples,
or heart, or inside my wrists?

What have you done to me,
love, when your absences
slow me down to inaction,
that slow metabolism of
despair, while your returnings
quicken my pulse excitedly,
the circulatory map of my
eager blood going to riot?

[c. 1983/84]

BREAD-AND-WATER WEEKEND

If my beloved should forsake me
with harsh words and goodbyes,
leave me unaccommodated by the world
from behind great bars of glass and iron,
then, how can my days be filled with feasts
though it is the height of June, and every
where blooms green...

                              Sweet is the balmy air
above the lake.

If my beloved place this world's affairs
before me, leaving me a forgotten relative
in the rural and faraway town of my loneliness,
where rivers of tears and memory run, their
histories unchronicled by the bright city lights
of his eyes, or fertile hands of his note-taking —

if he should leave me thus —

                              with the long thread
of the hours and a Spinning Jenny waiting
and patient in my room; with my larders empty,
and my pockets full of holes; with a cold
hard loaf and a jug of water —

if he should leave me thus —

how much more slowly can I die?

[c. 1983/84]

HOUSE NUMBER THIRTEEN

In a terrible dream,
I do not cry.

Sweet Jesus!
I have come not
to praise but to weep
before your gentle eyes.

A flood is needed to wash away this
deed, this hurt.
To wash away the murderer.

Still, I cannot weep. These edifices
of dreams continue to crumble.
A bomb was flung. The smoke
still rises from my head.

People pass on the street.
They see ruins and smoke.
They do not know who lived here,
with whom. They do not know
how it ended –

in a blast.

There was fire too.
Firemen put that out.

There will be no funeral.
It's too costly.

Survivors move to Chicago.
Or Washington.

A baby died here.
They saved themselves.
It was too late to save her,
they said with regret.

I come to pray for them all.
Murdered, and murderers, all.
I come to weep before
your gentle eyes,
sweet jesus.

[c. 1984/85]

SEA-WAIF

She was a creature
of Atlantic moonlight –
Essequibian, ethereal,
slight as a shadow.

When moon's full eye
opened wide over silver
sea, she appeared
in a dress that, soft
as a seabreeze, blew
about her knees.

She roamed bare stretches
between ocean and land.
She sought shells
to string a necklace,
one special shell.

Such a boneflower
placed by her ear
would yield sea-music –
a faint humming –
some sea-harp playing
from seabottom.

This curved quest was hers
whose fulfilment could so
easily be flung
from sea to sandy breast.

When moon was full
as a young mother's breast,
when sea was waved

with silver light, she appeared
each night, one week a season.

She spirited this beach, solitarily,
her soft hair blowing inwards,
like a tide from the sea.
Eyes downwards cast, she sought
some missing ornament, some shell
with music, a rare pearl
cast up from the deep —

a lonely fisherman, returning
from sea, weary,
with empty boat and net.

They called her 'sea-waif'.
Villagers told her tale
upon a silver midnight…

A child of fifteen — barely —
when she spirited this beach.
Her father was a fisherman,
with boats, net, a quick mind
and a lucky hand.

Motherless, she was.
Each day discovered her
playing on the sands.

Those castles of their promises
were her best friends.

Often, she gathered sea-shells
in her skirt's basket, her count
as careful as any miser's his gold.

Shell by shell,
she'd lay them down
upon the sand, a girlish
shell-vendor spreading her wares
before her great buyer, the sea.

Shell by shell,
she'd raise them
up, to set them down
again, these dead music-snails
upon the yielding sand.

Patient, in the evening,
she awaited fishing-boats.

Among these, her proud flagship –
that sailing palace bearing
her father home!

Father and daughter
reunited, going home
with the catch, nets
trailing behind.

A small hut, palm-covered,
their humble destination where
she'd prepare his supper –
her late mother's habit.

There too, she'd light
Grandpa's jug-lamp.
Its flames flickered
on the mud-baked walls.

Villagers called her
'little beach-comber' –

a sea-waif with a fortune —
in shells.

Sometimes, amused, they'd
watch her reprimand the sea.
'You should have fetched me
finer shells today!'

But soon
was she consoled
with one bright shell,
one special form, one perfect
twist of seabone.

Until that day the sea
swallowed father, boats,
nets and all.

Her grief was rage against
a wild monster that devoured
her sole parent without a trace
of sorrow, guilt or evidence.

Next day, the sea was itself
again, lapping wave after quiet
wave, calm and innocent.

Never had it yielded her
a finer batch of shells!

No one knew
what she said
to the sea.

No one
knew how it answered her.

Soon after her father's drowning,
she was seen no more.

Early one morn,
her childish form
was washed ashore:
a rare sea-shell surrendered
by that sea, at last.

She roams that stretch,
each season since,
her dress about her blowing
like a feather in seabreeze,
her hair streaming inwards
like a seatide, her eyes,
downwards cast –

as if she were seeking
some thing she was not finding.

Often, in a careful pause,
she'd stop, a shell held
erstwhile to her ear.

But those long-promised sea-harps
her father said she'd hear
seemed not to be playing.

Sadly, she'd move on,
seeking always some perfect one.

Till now, my friends,
such a perfect one
she has not found.

[c. 1984/85]

MICHEL, MICHEL

(in memory of a clay-baby from childhood)

In Babylon
you'd be a brick
made of straw
for the pyramids, Michel.

Thousands would come to gaze
at you and your brothers –
What a family in eternity!
Nobody would know it was you.

In heaven,
you'd be an angel.
Perhaps it was you, not Gabriel,
who wrestled with Elishah.

I can imagine such a plot
on your part for immortality!
For all the world cares, it was
Gabriel, not you, Michel.

But it seems you were subject
to larger ambitions.
Christ-mas was not good enough
for you, so it became
Michael-mas for your schemes!

A season after you, Michel!

But you were made
for a day,
you puny mud-baby –
so be content!

Stay in the dust, Michel!

Just so we loved
mon frère's little clay-boat.

Now it's done for!

(So why ask for more?)

Dream, clay and memory, Michel,
you're unmade.

You're unmade!

[c. 1984/85]

THE FLYING HORSEMAN

You are my knight,
Angel of death?
You are my Prince?

You've returned
from victory?
Are all enemies dead?

My lord, my lord,
you are so brave!

What *could* they do,
but die, Winged Mongol,
when you razed them to the ground?

My Lord, you are invincible.
They are quite dead!

Your flying horse
Rides without any legs.

You are my magic horseman
Galloping on the air.

Your cudgel scatters death
from on high. Your gifts
are deadly, sir;
shall I take them?

Would I spend my life in grief?

Would I lose a limb?

Would I love your black heart,
but then,

I'm not the E-N-E-M-Y!

[c. 1984/85]

PRINCE OF DEATH

Sea is open-wide.
The ship is beached.
Will the captain come forth?

Sky is desert-blue,
stars, fragments of ancient
moonchariots. The old planet of love
is cracked. Will the conqueror rise
out of his rocket?

The Tiger of Bengal is extinct.
The lion's mane singed to a stubble.
The black cat is declawed.

Will the Lord of the Forest come forth?

Sky's azure carpet, is it
still forested by stars?

No more the trilling
of those high nightingales?

Is the forest still emeraldine?

No fairy with a wand?

No high-riding prince?

No wedding at the story's end?

Come then, Black Sentinel.
shoulder your ghostly stars well!

Your ranks may salute them.
Fly above Plains of Death, Prince!
Ride above a Sea of Tears.

Flying high in your death-dealing
chariot, how can women's tears matter
to you? Death-bringer, your heart's

dressed-in-black.

The metal drone of death
screams near those orient martyrs
bulldozed on their land.

Unfurling your pirate masts
upon my open seas, you camp
under the Blue Roof of Heaven,

as if it were yours!

Pirate Invader!

Does your carrion fleet
hover, in mid-air
awaiting my corpse?

Are their wings
folded on the rock,
beaks hung
in low patience
upon the hull?

Gruesome lids flicker slowly
on my lonely horizons.

Did they come with you from Vietnam?

Are they still hungry,
O Minstrel of Kali?

Did you not feed them enough?

[c. 1984/85]

FRIEND,

if to me, you will no longer be tender,
nor touch my face with your eyes,
nor let your lips brush my hand –
how can I remain your friend?

You greet me as if I'm a stranger,
shaking my hand, never looking
my way. You talk to others,
leaving me out of your day.

How am I your friend
when you hate me so?

The baby cries into the telephone
before you come to greet me.
She is not ashamed of her demands.

[c. 1984/85]

THE VAMP'S PRIZE

A brassy belt girded
her waist as impossibly
as her ringed and smoke-filled
intentions about the New Year Ball.

Her arms were costume-jewelled,
a rapier of gold along her elbow,
a sword of silver by her hip.
On her fingers were all the rings
of forgotten Cleopatras....

Her fifty-five-year breasts
in skintight blacks,
sagged under the strain to stand erect.

Jetblack curls were too perfect
a piece. Beneath her folding
chin more jewels could be
hidden, or make-up end its
telltale mark in a comfortable crevice.

Her chin rose high
in the music-filled air.
A glittering purse
(with her secrets
of Methuselah) swung
with a measured swing
from her wrist.

Shiny earrings dangled
like last year's Christmas
decorations from her ear.

Community fathers
and the holy brotherhood
froze as she catwalked the length
of their fundraiser. Green
lucre laughed from her cleavage
as fullsuited fathers and tasteful
wives, obedient sons and girlfriends
turned their gaze away.

She didn't win, not a single
prize. A ragamuffin with a torn
denim at the knee, cheeks
ruddy as a rural filly,
carried the crown.

After, women scorned "the vamp",
staring hard at the money
down her breasts, her
smoky kohl-drawn eyes.

Downing a gay whisky, she
ignored them. A long cigarette,
theatrically held between her
ringed fingers, smoked
like a genie into night's promised air.

As I left an empty hall,
a last lavender balloon in my hand,
I saw that loser remove her shiny pumps,
then slowly, without prime prize or flesh,
limp into New Year morning.

[c. 1985]

DEATH OF THE FLOWER-MAIDEN

A jewelled pouch
by his hips strung,
a sword and a sickle:
Death rides in the moonlight
on a fine black horse.

Has he robbed your cradle?
Has he robbed your bed?

Have you seen him in the moonlight
have you seen him ride

a cape from his shoulders flowing
black in the wind, eyes masked
in the devilish light?

Boots to his thighs, a sickle
by his side – behold,

Death rides
in the magical night.

By life's twilight plains,
deserted after daylight, this pale rider
canters by.

Deserted by the living,
deserted by the dead,
only Death breathes in eery light.
Death only breathes when his horseman rides by.

Has he passed by your window?
Has he knocked at your door?

If you've dreamt of a horseman
with a musical gallop, riding in moonlight
with a sword and a sickle –

Beware!

Eyes masked against the night,
Death rides!

If he taps at your window,
slam your shutters!
If he comes by your backdoor,
drive him away!

Do not invite that gentleman in –
he will woo you till
he steals your heart away!

He speaks of a land beyond sorrows,
a land beyond tears;
he tells of milk-and-honey trees,
and music, ripe pollen in the air.

He says you'll never want
for food, or for love.
He tells of harmonies
and everlasting loves.

He'll give you babies
by the dozen, and honey
by the gallon.

He'll sing to you – then –
away with you he'll ride
across the land of the living
to the Land beyond sorrow.

He says: 'I take you
to my Land of Love and Honey...'
(You will protest,
but he'll never let you go.)

Death's a faithful lover.
He will never let you go.

'I must bid adieu
to my loved ones...
I have some cheese to make;
I have to make some butter...'

Death will not stop
despite your urgent tone.

'Wait. I must tell Grandma
this fate which befalls me...'

Why did she not listen
when I told her my dream:
a man-in-moonlight riding,
a jewelled pouch by his hip,
a sword and a sickle?

(In silver moonlight,
eyes masked against the world,
he rode a black horse
through the magical night.)

Ten years ago,
I saw your silhouette on the hilltop,
as I played in a poppy-field,
a frisky young girl.

I showed you to Mama.
She said, 'Hush, don't tell lies.'
I said, 'There's a man-on-horseback, Mama.'

She would not look.
Nor would she listen.

'There's supper to be ate,' she said,
leading me home.

I turned. I looked again.
'Oh Mama, he is gone!'
I wept all evening.
I wouldn't eat my supper.

Mama sang me songs.
Mama gave me many toys.

But I recalled the man-on-horseback
with boots to his thighs,
a cape from his shoulders flowing
high in the wind.

These things I remembered
as I rode by his side; this
man-in-the-moonlight
with boots to his thighs.

Cantering across the skylight,
he had come in my dreams,
his shadow flickering
on lonely nights.

'I am he you have dreamt of,'
he said to me at last;
'I am the man-in-the-moonlight

who stood on the hilltop.
My name is Death.
I have come for you at last.

'You never were ready
but I have waited so long.
I have watched you from the hilltop.
I have beckoned to you.

'I have waited in the shadows
as you wept for me.

'I take you, my dear,
to a land of always-moonlight
where stars shine all day
and suns burn all night.
You go into day as you wish,
or night as you please, and
angels come to elucidate
your harmonies.

'A place where food is milk
and honey, a place to dwell
without fear, where good
is always present, where good
is always near.'

'Take me there' she cried
in ecstasy. 'I cannot wait
to get there.'

'Take time, my dear maiden,
to reflect on the past. We're
passing through a twilight zone
between your new home and the last.

'Your Mama is still in tears.
She has lost her treasure.
Your Mama is overwrought.
Think of her sorrow.

'Your Grandma is old.
She keeps wagging her head.
She knew your fate before you did,
for you told her your dreams.

'She breathed not a word,
for it was not fit to say.
Your Mama would have jailed you,
if she knew she'd lose you this way.

'Your brother mourns
for his playmate. He'll miss you;
but in time he'll find another,
so do not fear.

'Your sweetheart is penitent.
He has driven you to death.
He knows not this appointment
to which you were sent.

'I gathered you from the edge
of the city. Abandoned by your sweetheart,
you had frozen all night. Winter's
not fit to throw a tantrum, dear,
but what does it matter?

'I take you now to the land
of always-moonlight, the land
beyond sorrow, the land beyond tears.'

[c.1984]

SILENT MY HEART

Silent, my heart.
She will take him in good care.
See how tightly he holds
her hand.

He is sleeved, this wintry
afternoon, in black, and
scarfed in homely plaid,
a girl hangs on his arm.
She may be his wife.

Hush, my heart.
You knew him when he walked
against the cold wind, coatless,
lost, like a small-town boy with
faraway eyes in a big impersonal city.

She will care for him.

He won't buy many sandwiches now.
The deli-people will be sad.

After home-made suppers,
nights beside glowing-red
candles; after she's hung
his shirts in the bathroom,
stayed up with him as he
writes his book —

he won't lack for company.

You were never in the picture,
my girl, you were an extra
who thought herself a star.

A dream, nonetheless.

So hush my heart.
Be happy he's found her
to sit with him near home-fires.
One good and true;
one to bear his child.

[c. 1984/85]

UNTITLED

I am not clear
how you opened the door,
but you let me out.

How is a rose removed,
interim hope, glassy-held, not for long,
from its stem to the trash?

The wild wind of fashion arrested your eye.
How did it give birth to a change-of-address?
How was I rendered obsolete?

Older than a year, a fad, a whim,
a summer's short love, I am grown
away from childhood, daughter lost
by the disintegration of fatherhoods,
sister exiled from a dream, lover deceased.

What wind was this which my gods sent by you?

[c. 1985/86]

ON TEDDY-BEARS (& LITTLE GIRLS)

I'd rather write a poem than a paper –
no doubt.
Teddy here agrees wholeheartedly!

I'd rather wear no knickers
than a pinstripe suit.
Here again,
Teddy's and my opinions merge,
in synchronicity!

A tidy thing – a toy –
faithful hopes of children –
and of a certain little girl who
once was –
(is she any more?)

She had longhaired dolls.
She had baby pots.
She had tidy brothers.
Cowboys and homebodies all,
they had quite some fun.
No doubt.

It's a different world now.
I'd say.
Papers, four months rent due,
a roommate who's no longer a roommate
(but must remain a roommate nevertheless),

with a dream that's turned into myth –
some distant star – Jupiter perhaps,
or Mars. I dare not mention Venus.

Strange life.

Little girls are presumed to have grown up
some time ago,
grown wise enough to subvert the wolf.
Even if they're in the woods,
all on their lonesome — and
the woodman died long ago.

It's just another distant star —
another myth.

Stranger still.
Little girls who might speak so well,
do not speak up!
The wolf eats them up!

It never was a world for little girls
and baby dolls.
Whoso said it was, was wrong.
Himself a wolf or saint.

Look at Teddy here.
Once a reassuring toy,
now by your bed (knickerless,
you pointed out)
with a wicked grin
on that dyed splayed rope
I used to think was fur!

[c. 1986]

BLUE VIOLINS

A moon of purple hangs in the nightsky.
Oh, acidic-hued days of my gloom,
threatening rain of sorrow overburdening
the roof! Sweet daughters of day,
come loosen your long hair of Spring
before me. Sing in those flutelike voices
of promises of sun. The blue violins of sadness
are playing.

[c. 1986]

BARRED

All is barred.

Only my voice
may climb your stair.
Are you listening?

Is it you who hold
this power of God?
Is it you who can let me in?

Step by step
upon the carpeted stair, I creep,
fingers to my lips,
one foot in front of another.

Did I come to see you unshaven?

Did this draw me up your stairs
like a moon to the sun's magnet
into the blue-green orbit of your eyes?

At the foot of your door, I stare,
dwarfed by man's constructions
upon the blue air.

[c. 1986]

WATCHING

Already, I have dreamt of you.
Dark curls and gentle demeanour.
In my dreams, you hold me in forbidden places.
I long for night.

I am being called away.
Silently, you beckon,
awaiting my answer.

[c. 1986]

MUSICAL BEDS

That night, I slept in yours,
you in mine; I in your arms,
you in mine entangled.

Sleep came and went.
Beds were exchanged, like rooms.
Still we sought each other,
angry or no,

two beds or not —

it was one which found us
inevitably entwined, together
reconciled.

[c. 1986]

UNTITLED

Look at me:
when you speak,
mountain ranges
rise inside me.

[c. 1986]

PRE-TRIAL DAYS

In a black satchel of tears,
I hide the broken pieces
of my crystal urn.

O people of this town!

I seek a glass-blower.
My pieces must be melted
to their first wax.

Lend me your craftsman.
Hire him to me for a day.
He must be the finest artisan,
a priest devoted to his art
pure in heart in spirit
like Christ to the poor
Michelangelo to David,
Gandhi, an artist divine.

I bring my assaulted ears
in search of your poets,
for the drums of these
listening trees have been felled

[c. 1986]

MONDAY, COME QUICKLY

Come quickly, Monday.
Your flag in my heart hides
from the wind of his eyes.

Deep-flung, I drink turquoise
pools of sudden water.
I am a mermaid basking on the rock
of his glance.

Woman-at-sea, I am vine-bound
upon rafters of his smile.

The razor-teeth of the hours,
swift, sure sharks, lurk
beneath my bark.

Light shards from above.

Nights of his absence
seem distant.

IN THE CLEAR BALLROOM...

In the clear ballroom of your eyes,
I dance, my skirts hemmed in by
bright ribbons of your smiles.

Charmed
by the warm waltz of your caress,
love's musical pulse –
a time-insistent rhythm that snatches
my heart like a beat in wild metric bars –
I swirl, I sway in that gaze – gracefully.

Love, love,
were you here,
would my gown
still billow in your eyes?

SWITCH OFF THE DARKNESS

Switch off the darkness, sweet.
Direct your smile with its rosedrawn
chariots across my dark clouds.
I need your light, young one –
not a small star, some dim moon
nightly sliced in my sky,
but your whole golden coin
so I may freely spend it
across love's counter in your eyes.

THE COMING OF THE MAIDEN

Upon a sea of violins, in the symphonic air
Rode a majestic swan in splendour
Beneath a choir of stars!

Upon blue Atlantic waters, with high-raised wing,
Floated the Secret Lake's white bird.
Sleekly, this slender maiden

To shellpink coral islands, in blue Caribbean,
Glided this long-tressed brown maiden
Asleep, above her watery world.

She floated to Antigua, a small English pearl,
Stranded bead by glistening bead upon
blue blue Caribbean.

[c. 1986]

BERNINI BABY

Black-booted,
he glistened in brass,
officious as a policeman.

He flung a greeting – a glance
at my breast, a parcel at my foot;
clicked his boot, and left.

A bomb carefully packaged,
it lay, waiting to boom

into my dreams, curly-haired,
of mother's return...

*

A woman examining her meat
at the butcher's, I poke at it.
Poke and stir. Poke and stir.
I can feel its planks
under brown paper.

Butterflies break loose
inside.

One sharp stroke –
the tape's cut clean!

(Neither sea's saltness
nor my ship's opaque darkness
has hurt her, I hope.)

I fuss and I fuss
over this box.
Is it my delivery?

An Atlantic crossing
accomplished on my birthday –

it's a Bernini baby
in her nest!

I knew she was coming,
a girl presuming to call
herself – C-A-N-D-I-E
(despite my wishes
she be named for one
holy or royal – she's Candie!)

Candie, Candie
you're a gift
I cannot return or exchange,
but besides the fact that the stores
wouldn't take you – you're a bargain!
I'm keeping you!

You're fragile, you're exquisite,
you cost me a fortune.
I'm keeping you!

Lifted from a baby-blue bassinet,
sweet *objet d'art*, you smile at me,
wings folded in winter.

Swaddling cloths are wrapped,
muslins of stone around you.

[c. 1986]

LAMENT

Johnnie, oh Johnnie,
my beau's gone away,
without word, without promise,
without kissing me adieu.

He flew from me
like a mateless robin in summer.
It may have been Friday.
It may have been Monday.

He's gone a-romeoing in Paris
in long French avenues,
avec cette fille ou cette fille,
très jolie, très jeune.

He says he works fine mornings,
paying tribute to Galileo –
that I know and believe,
but the rest – I don't know!

What shall I do, Johnnie,
shall I scour maps of la France,
pensant des belles chambres
avec cette fille ou cette fille,
très jolie, très jeune –
avec beaucoup de savoir-faire,
avec beaucoup de charmes.

Johnnie, oh Johnnie
please take me to the zoo.
I'll feed this broken heart
to the lions, the striped cats,
the caymans.

He doesn't love me, Johnnie,
il ne m'aime pas!

I may never come knocking
at your office door.
Weeds may grow roof-high
at the place where my heart's
green plant once stood.

Ivy may cover walls
outside your window,
creeping inch on inch
by their tiny feet.

You may grow old,
you may grow a beard,
I might become a doddering lady
tapping her memories out,
step by step.

You may change your job.
You may marry
and move out west
against the frontier of my heart.

How could I reach you,
you will have moved so far?

If I came on horseback
if I came on Pegasus
would I find you?
Would you be there?

I may never come again
to the seventh floor,
eagerly pressing the elevator
buttons to your heart.

As far as my heart goes,
these poems were a lift,
rising. With me trapped inside,
the lift stuck.

Had I rung the alarm,
had I pushed the panic-button,
would you have heard me?
Would you have been there
to rescue me?

Monsieur, oh monsieur,
buy me a kerchief
my love has left me,
but tears have not.

Monsieur, oh monsieur,
sit down for a while
by this summer branch
and tell me, oh tell
me of old Paris.

'It's a gay city.
Romance is by far
the light that looms largest
in that town's repertoire!'

Monsieur, oh monsieur,
sit a while longer
and tell me do tell
what you mean by that smile.

'I mean, my dear, no more
and no less. It's a great
place for love, child.
I know that for sure.'

Monsieur, oh monsieur,
my love's just gone there!
Tell me oh tell me
will he be the same

as other gentlemen
who, leaving their town,
find, in a new city,
an even newer love?

'What can I say, child,
though I am now old,
I, too, was handsome,
adventurous, bold,

seeking new cities,
fresh sights and fresh loves –
if your guy is young
and as keen as I was,

then – his song's sung, dear,
he'll do just the same!
He'll chase pretty faces
he'll ride in slow boats

with pretty things
on wise, old, blue Seine!
He'll kiss and kiss them
and say that he cares –

but he may leave them,
like men do sometimes.
Perhaps he may find
one who's more special
to his dreams, his ambitions.

She knows – all at once –
that she's found him,
who's found her – then
what can you do, dear?
They'll both fall in love!'

Monsieur, oh Monsieur,
you say such mean things.
Perhaps you wish
he'll meet this woman.'

'My child, my child,
I wish no such link.
Mildly, I tell you –
I merely say what I think.

He has travelled
to Raphaelite Paris.
I only warn you
of dangers ahead.'

Monsieur, oh monsieur,
I didn't mean to say…
but thanks all the same.
Now what is my game?

My love's recently
gone there and I've
not heard one note since
from that migrant bird!

'Child, do not worry,
don't worry so much.
Spend some time in temples.
Spend some time at home.

And, do not chat
with any man you see.
This city's dangerous –
more than that one out there!

Your love may return
as true as his eyes.
You may not greet him,
if you are not wise!

Return to safe streets.
Return to your home.
Visit quiet temples
and, please, do not roam!

Your love may not be,
as you think him to be,
chasing after ladies
and making new babies!

He may be that kind who
Is different from I.
He may be the one
with the truest eyes!'

[c. 1986]

THE LEAF IN HIS EAR

For Charlie

Left, the golden leaf bears from his ear.
At eighteen, Bushman fighting to control diamonds
in his glass head. The waters of the river
swirl by.

I and I Rastaman, with knotty India hair, has long ago ceased.
The good Lord swallowed him up.
Into Guiana forests. North-west.
Dogs bark and howl.
In this first of May day, the Almighty is rain,
voices, wind in banana suckers.

LUCKY

Down at the bottom of the river, the fishes
swirl around his ears. Lucky hunts for gold.
Away from the teeming world of city streets
and crying wives, he meditates on God and his world.

The white man from England tugs twice
on the water-hole of his mask. Simultaneously,
God tugs Lucky. An electric eel, smoothly, snakelike
touches him.

A current moves like lightning
from the back of the eel's head to his ankle.
"Ouch!" is torn from my father's lips. He
swims frantically up towards shore.

LEARNER

I am the great learner.
I devour the apple but before that,
I halve, then quarter
and eighth it.

I am a baby feeding on mashed yams.
I discover red apples and green ones,
small apples, large ones. Romanos,
Granny Smiths.

I have eaten them.
Flame in the gut. Like a Chinese dragon,
I hold horses, I drive and I breathe fire.
Adam and Eve in one, I am in a garden,
eating. Breathing.
There are raspberries too, and bananas.
The banana-man sells me some.

I, oriental fire-dragon, mother Kali
in China, wrap snakes around my neck and
eat the fruits, belching out ribbons of fire
into the snow-white prison to which I am
relegated.
Bars are white hot iron.
Books encased in cartons stand low
against the bars.

TEARS

Bones of dew scatter on my plate
as they rain down the land.
How can I stop them? They splatter
through my dreams leaving me homeless.
Oh God! I am naked as a newborn.
I implore you with my tears.

ANT AND ETERNITY

I.

A tiny ant walked on my book's side as
I struggled to read one page.
With my big human mouth, I blew it away,
or tried to.
Hurtly, it swaggered. Then,
I was remorseful.
I let it come and read my page.
After all, it had known the book-tree millions
of years before my birth.

II.

On the stairs of the green old house,
I hurried to enter, but I desired to house
your house with my rubber company.
You refuse to house my hand or water plants growing boarish
from my nostrils. Instead, you said, *Go ahead. But beware.*
There's a lone ant on the step!

III.

I saw a lone ant
and I wondered whither were its companions.
Where was the battalion? Under the earth?
Suddenly, three ants appealed to me,
on my tabletop with clasped hands, bodies straight up.

IV.

Had the blue god and his wife sent them to me?
Will loneliness be the land of my sojourn?
And, having done their job, the three ants disappeared.

V.

Sister, are you my sister?
Ajee, your love is immense.

A love with a camel's hump riding through the swirling sands
of my fate.

MURDERED

A crimson sun drowns over Guyana horizons
at dusk.
Birds do not chatter but droop.
Dogs howl.
News is a young girl raped and murdered
in Le Repentir graveyard of impenitence.
The whole country mourns like fathers
and mothers weeping open-eyed.
What has become of citizens responsible
for their brothers?
Like Cain, the killer slays his blood

[c. 1994]

RETURN ME TO THE FIRE
RETURN ME TO MYSELF

If I should ever die
Return me to the fire
If I should live again
Return me to myself.
Heartfire,
        flame in hurricane-lamp
Outside, into this storm.

[June 1990]

INDEX OF FIRST LINES

ABOUT THE AUTHOR

Mahadai Das was born in Eccles, East Bank Demerara, Guyana in 1954. She wrote poetry from her early school days at Bishops High School, Georgetown. She completed her first degree at the University of Guyana and received her MA at Columbia University, New York, and then began a doctoral program in Philosophy at the University of Chicago. There, Das became ill and never completed the programme. In Guyana, she'd been a dancer, actress, teacher, and beauty-queen, served as a volunteer member of the Guyana National Service in c1976 and was part of the Messenger Group promoting 'Coolie' art forms at a time when Indo-Guyanese culture was virtually excluded from national life.

As a young poet, Das published her first pieces in *KAIE*, the official literary publication of Guyana's History and Arts Council, as well as in other local publications. Her first collection, *I Want to be a Poetess of My People* (1977), traced the roots of the Guyanese people from slavery and indentureship to independence. The collection calls for a new identity independent of colonial powers, though it also bears the marks of being beholden to the sloganizing politics of the time. Her second collection of poetry, *My Finer Steel Will Grow* (1982), expresses bleak disillusionment with the corruption and authoritarianism that had overtaken the nationalist project. In her third collection, *Bones* (Peepal Tree, 1988), Das addresses her experiences as an Indo-Caribbean woman living in the materialistic culture of the urban USA.

Mahadai Das was, with Rajkumari Singh, one of the first Indo-Guyanese women writers to speak to both the ethnic and gender issues facing Indo-Caribbean women, though there are never simple or fixed identifications of identity in her work. *I Want to be a Poetess of my People* speaks of her Indian heritage within a broad Caribbean environment, yet speaks little of her experience as a woman. *My Finer Steel Will Grow* attempts to reconcile the individual with the political with regard to gender. She speaks about the discrepancy in fighting with men for political freedom, only to be suppressed by those same men in personal relationships. *Bones* explores her changing individual female identity, but only in two or three poems incorporates her

Indian heritage within this identity. It is clear that Das was determined never to be coralled into any fixed position.

Over the last decade of her life, Mahadai Das suffered from debilitating health problems. These curtailed the writing career of one of the Caribbean's most talented women poets. In April 2003 her life came to a tragically early end.